# PHalarope Books

PHalarope books are designed specifically for the amateur naturalist. These volumes represent excellence in natural history publishing. Each book in the PHalarope series is based on a nature course or program at the college or adult education level or is sponsored by a museum or nature center. Each PHalarope book reflects the author's teaching ability as well as writing ability. Among the books:

*The Wildlife Observer's Guidebook*
Charles E. Roth

*The Plant Observer's Guidebook: A Field Botany Manual for the Amateur Naturalist*
Charles E. Roth

*Suburban Wildlife: An Introduction to the Common Animals of Your Back Yard and Local Park*
Richard Headstrom

*Suburban Wildflowers: An Introduction to the Common Wildflowers of Your Back Yard and Local Park*
Richard Headstrom

*Botany in the Field: An Introduction to Plant Communities for the Amateur Naturalist*
Jane Scott

*Wood Notes: A Companion and Guide for Birdwatchers*
Richard H. Wood

*The Curious Naturalist*
John Mitchell and the Massachusetts Audubon Society

*Trees: An Introduction to Trees and Forest Ecology for the Amateur Naturalist*
Laurence C. Walker

# A FIELD GUIDE TO THE FAMILIAR

*Learning to Observe
the Natural World*

## GALE LAWRENCE

*Illustrated by Adelaide Murphy*

A SPECTRUM BOOK

*Prentice-Hall, Inc., Englewood Cliffs, New Jersey 07632*

*Library of Congress Cataloging in Publication Data*

Lawrence, Gale, (date).
   A field guide to the familiar.

(PHalarope books)
   "A Spectrum Book."
   Bibliography: p.
   Includes index.
   1. Biology—Field work.   2. Nature study.   I. Murphy,
Adelaide.   II. Title.
QH318.5.L39   1984        574'.072        83–24558
ISBN 0–13–314071–7
ISBN 0–13–314063–6 (pbk.)


ISBN 0-13-314071-7

ISBN 0-13-314063-6 {PBK.}

This book is available at a special discount when ordered
in bulk quantities. Contact Prentice-Hall, Inc., General
Publishing Division, Special Sales, Englewood Cliffs, N.J. 07632.

10  9  8  7  6  5  4  3  2  1
Printed in the United States of America

Editorial/production supervision by Chris McMorrow
Interior design by Joan Ann Jacobus
Cover design by Hal Siegel
Manufacturing buyers: Edward J. Ellis and Doreen Cavallo


Prentice-Hall International, Inc., *London*
Prentice-Hall of Australia Pty. Limited, *Sydney*
Prentice-Hall Canada Inc., *Toronto*
Prentice-Hall of India Private Limited, *New Delhi*
Prentice-Hall of Japan, Inc., *Tokyo*
Prentice-Hall of Southeast Asia Pte. Ltd., *Singapore*
Whitehall Books Limited, *Wellington, New Zealand*
Editora Prentice-Hall do Brasil Ltda., *Rio de Janeiro*

*T*his book is dedicated to Bob Spear, who already knows
what I'm trying to learn and never makes me feel ignorant.

# CONTENTS

## WINTER, MORE WINTER, AND WAITING

## BEGINNING TO BE SPRING

## SPRING

# INTRODUCTION

$M$ost field guides are designed to help you figure out what you don't know. This field guide is different. It begins with what you do know and encourages you to learn more.

It is a field guide in the sense that it will lead you into—or back into—the field to look more closely at things that are already familiar to you, but it breaks from the traditional field-guide format in several ways. First, instead of isolating classes of natural phenomena and following evolutionary order or similarities in appearance, it intermixes subjects and follows the seasons. Second, it offers essays rather than abbreviated, formulaic information. And finally, it is not just a reference book but a suggested model for learning about the natural world.

There is purpose here. My approach is, on the one hand, more elementary than that of standard field guides, and, on the other, more advanced.

It is more elementary in that it reflects the way an untrained mind works. When someone who has never before paid attention to the natural world suddenly starts looking, the field seems a bewildering array of plants, animals, stars, seasons, weather conditions, scenes, and feelings. The natural world is whole and continuous—and, for many beginners, unapproachable.

Before these beginners will be able to use standard field guides, they must learn to focus on plants and animals one at a time. They must also develop habits of close observation that will enable them to make the distinctions field guides call for. The essays in this book are designed to promote habits and attitudes appropriate for a thoughtful naturalist.

At the other end of the learning process, my approach is more advanced than that of standard field guides. I move beyond field guides to encourage naturalists to reintegrate what they have distinguished and identified in the field. By focusing on common things and showing how much more there is to know about them than their names, I challenge naturalists to carry their learning beyond field identification into an awareness of interrelationships, life processes, and seasonal behaviors.

Every plant and animal—and even every nonliving phenomenon—has its story. Plants and animals must live, die, eat, mate, compete, defend, and accommodate. Things that are not alive—a rainbow, for instance, or a shooting star—have their stories too, their histories and explanations. All these stories are important because they interact with one another and with the human story.

By juxtaposing the different life forms (as well as a few nonliving things) and moving through the year, I invite naturalists to be alert to everything in all seasons. It may be romantic, but in my own learning I have pretended that I'm living in earlier, prescientific times, when people who noticed anything noticed everything—with the difference, of course, that I can draw on the wealth of information made available by generations of scientists who have dedicated their lives to specialized research.

This book is in no way intended as a substitute for the many excellent field guides available today. It is, rather, an introduction for those who aren't ready to use field guides yet and a supplement for those who use field guides but want to know more. It is based on my own discoveries of the natural world and my readings of the scientific literature. I offer it to fellow naturalists—beginners and otherwise—as a service, an encouragement, and a sharing of what I have learned.

I would like to acknowledge the assistance of Peter Wagner, who read the entire manuscript thoughtfully and sensitively, Deborah Bouchard, who typed the entire manuscript, and Joan Cannizzaro, who proofread parts of it.

# FIRST FROST AND INDIAN SUMMER

# FROST
## Learning to Observe the Atmosphere

*W*hy would a book about nature begin with the first frost? Doesn't the natural year begin traditionally with spring, when plants are breaking their winter dormancy and birds are migrating northward to nest? The problem for an observer of the natural world is that the year never begins or ends anywhere. Natural events just keep happening, changing with the seasons, continuing, overlapping, and following ancient sequences that have more to do with the sun than with calendars.

The first frost is a clear ending of sorts, but it's also a beginning. More than any other natural event, it's an edge or dividing time that we can record each year as a point of reference. In New England, the killing frost—the one that turns the last vulnerable plants to seaweed—usually comes in late September or early October.

It's easy to think of this frost as nothing more than frozen dew, but it's actually a somewhat different phenomenon. If it were frozen dew, it should look like frozen dewdrops, but frost is crystalline, more closely akin to snow. On plants the crystalline structure is difficult to see, but if you look closely at frost on a windowpane, you will perceive its delicate feathery edges. When you scrape the frost off your car windshield, it will look even more like snow as it falls from your scraper. The white shavings could easily be packed into a little snowball.

Dew and frost both appear on clear, windless nights. When the air cools after the sun goes down, it can't hold as much moisture as it did during the day. In summer the moisture condenses, forming droplets of dew on the cool surfaces of plants, spider webs, tents, sleeping bags, and other exposed objects. Frost forms on similar still nights, but with one important difference— the temperature is below freezing. The same vapor that would have condensed into dew on a warmer night crystallizes into frost when the thermometer dips below 32° F (0° C).

The vapor that becomes frost does not first turn to water and then freeze. It changes directly from its invisible gaseous state into the crystalline form we see. This process is called *sublimation*. The same process works in reverse when you hang wet laundry outdoors in winter: the laundry freezes and then it dries. The frozen moisture in the clothing evaporates directly into the atmosphere without having to melt first.

Sometimes moisture moves through the cold night air as fog. You'd think that if the temperature of the air were below freezing, the fog's tiny water droplets would be frozen too, but they're not because water has the ability to be *supercooled*. That is, as long as the droplets are not disturbed, they can stay liquid at temperatures well below the freezing point. But it's a delicate balance. If the supercooled droplets encounter an object—like a tree, for instance—they can't resist the temperature any longer, and they crystallize all over the tree.

On a cold morning after a fog, we see this special kind of frost where the fog has passed. It is called *rime*. Rime is an accumulation of granular ice tufts on trees or other exposed objects that stood in the path of supercooled fog. The rime-covered trees of a mountain forest invite fantasies of ice palaces and fairy kingdoms.

Although fall is best known for its brilliant colors, these transient, crystalline whites play their part, too. The first frost, in addition to orienting us within the natural year, clears our senses and attunes us to the special days that lie ahead.

# ASTERS
## Learning to Look Closely
## at a Wild Flower

*F*all doesn't seem like the right time of year to think about wild flowers, but the brilliant shades of purple that wait until September and October to color the roadsides demand attention. An aster looks like a ready-made bouquet. Its numerous small flower heads, each resembling a miniature daisy, grow at the tips of a much-branched stem. Daisies, asters, and many of our other common wild flowers belong to the family of plants called *composites.* Each individual flower head is composed of numerous individual flowers. These individual flowers, which are difficult to perceive as flowers, are called *florets.*

The small, tightly packed florets in the center of the

aster's head are called *disk florets.* They are shaped like tubes, but if you look at them closely with a hand lens, you can see the flower parts that make each a complete flower. These disk florets, which are usually yellow in asters, have both male and female parts.

The thin flat flowers that radiate from the central disk florets are called *ray florets.* If you pull one out, you will see a little tuft of white around its base. These ray florets lack male parts, but they have female parts and can produce seeds. The white tuft is designed to help the seeds fly with the wind when they are mature and ready to disperse. Different species of asters have different color ray florets, but many are beautiful shades of purple, blue, and violet.

You must have steady fingers to play "He loves me, he loves me not" with an aster. Daisies are big enough to make the game easy, but asters test patience and manual dexterity. You must also be a determined counter. One small aster might present you with eighty ray florets and at least as many disks.

With so many ray and disk florets growing so close together, asters and other composites make it easy for insect pollinators to do their work. One pollen-laden butterfly, moth, bee, bumblebee, or fly can pollinate several florets during just one visit. Not all florets are ready to be pollinated at the same time, however. The female rays are usually ready to receive pollen first; then some of the disks begin to produce pollen to be carried to other flowers. Later, the disks present their female parts to insect pollinators. This careful timing is designed to prevent self-pollination. If you visit the same aster every day for a week or so, you can observe the gradual changes in the individual florets, and if you go out after dark with a flashlight, you will see the ray florets closed protectively over the pollen-bearing disks.

Most asters are perennial, so if you see them growing in a certain place this year, you can go back and watch for them to come up again next year. Some species produce their new plants in a clump right around the old plant, whereas others send out long underground stems that produce new plants at a distance from the old. Late in the fall asters, like all the other wild flowers that have come and gone, go to seed. Each flower head becomes a fuzzy little seed head offering hundreds of potential new asters to the fall winds.

The name *aster* comes from the Greek word for star. Our late fall "star flowers" provide us with one last opportunity to study wild flowers before everything turns to brown and brittle winter weeds.

# BUMBLEBEES
## Learning to Observe an Insect That Hibernates

Sometime during the fall—it's difficult to pinpoint exactly when—familiar insects just aren't around anymore. While you're observing your asters, keep an eye open for what might be your last glimpse of a bumblebee. Even after several frosts, you will still see and hear a few of them buzzing hungrily around late-blooming flowers. Summer's hard work is over for most bumblebees, but some individuals—the young females—still have a job to do. The future of the species depends on their ability to survive winter and produce eggs for a new colony next spring.

Bumblebees are like honeybees in many ways, but their

response to winter is significantly different. Honeybees store honey, and the whole colony withdraws into its well-stocked hive to take its chances on surviving winter together. Bumblebees, rather than worrying about the survival of the entire colony, concentrate their late summer effort on the queens. At the same time that the old queen lays eggs to produce her successors, she lays other eggs to produce a few males. Once the young males and females have left, the work of the old colony is done. The old bumblebees die without replacements, and eventually the whole colony just fades away.

While the colony is disintegrating, the young males spread out, each establishing a territory by leaving his scent on twigs and leaves. A young female detects the scent, enters the male's territory, and mates with him. Because all the colonies in an area are responding to the same seasonal cues, females have a good chance of encountering males who are not their brothers. One mating is all a female needs to prepare for her future. The males die shortly after they've mated, while the fertilized females continue to feed and fatten themselves for the long months of hibernation ahead. They will spend the winter buried in the earth in an inactive, almost deathlike state.

The females who survive winter become active again in April or May. They seek out early-blooming trees and wild flowers and stuff themselves with protein-rich pollen to help them produce their eggs. Each queen must also find a suitable home for the large family she will bear. Whereas honeybees build their hives in hollow trees or specially constructed boxes, bumblebees prefer the ground. A queen might move into a grassy nest left by a field mouse, or she might choose an underground burrow excavated by another animal.

In her chosen home, the queen builds a wax honeypot and fills it with regurgitated nectar. She also gathers pollen and lays her first batch of eight to ten eggs right on a pollen clump she has deposited on the floor. The eggs hatch in four to five days, and the queen mixes pollen with nectar to feed the larvae. For about a week or so the hungry larvae feed and grow. When they have attained their full size, they spin cocoons and pupate for another ten to fourteen days. When they emerge from their cocoons as adults, they are at first too wet and weak to fly outside, so they feed out of the queen's honeypot. Finally, after about two more days, they are ready to help the busy queen, who has already laid more eggs.

During most of the summer all the bumblebees that hatch from the queen's eggs are infertile females who function as workers. The older workers forage for food, while the younger ones help in the nursery. Only at the end of the summer does the queen produce fertile offspring.

Whereas honeybees—and, incidentally, human beings— store food to sustain their species through winter, bumblebees find it more efficient to invest their genes in a few individuals and then die. The only important thing for any species is to have a new generation started before the last of the old one dies.

# MONARCH BUTTERFLIES
## *Learning to Observe an Insect That Migrates*

*W*hereas bumblebees survive winter by producing queens that hibernate, monarch butterflies survive by producing a whole generation that migrates. The amazing thing about the monarchs' fall migration is that not one of the butterflies who makes it was alive the prior spring when the monarchs flew the other way. There are therefore no senior butterflies to lead or even to indicate the proper direction. But somehow the species manages to transmit the flight plan through four or five generations, and in the fall, monarchs head south.

Western monarchs head for the California coast. Millions of them congregate in a town called Pacific Grove, where they cluster in pine trees and create a local attraction. For years, however, the winter whereabouts of eastern monarchs was a mystery. Some of them were seen in Florida or traveling along the Gulf Coast, but there were never enough of them in any one place to account for the millions that had inhabited Canada and the eastern and central United States during the summer. It wasn't until 1975 that a researcher discovered the wintering ground of these missing monarchs. They were hiding out in the mountains of central Mexico, at an elevation of about 9,000 feet, where the climate was cool and moist, and where, before 1975, the only human activities were logging and cattle herding.

Now that this major wintering ground has been discovered, scientists are gradually piecing together the monarchs' story. Tags placed on the wings of the monarchs indicate that some of them have traveled all the way from Canada, from as far as 2,400 miles away, to spend the winter at or near this spot. New tags placed on the wings of the wintering monarchs indicate that some of them fly as far as 1,000 miles back north in the spring before they die. With large, sedentary aggregations of butterflies to observe, scientists are learning exactly what climatic conditions the insects have sought out, how they respond to variations in the weather, and what daylengths and temperatures start them mating and moving northward in the spring. They have also observed birds, cows, small mammals, and even human beings preying on these supposedly inedible butterflies.

With sheer numbers in their favor, many monarchs survive the flight south, winter weather, and predations to make at least part of the trip north again in the spring. Most of them mate before they leave their Mexican wintering ground, and many of the males die soon thereafter. The fertilized females lay their eggs on the emerging milkweeds they encounter in northern Mexico and the southern United States. These old females fly northward as long as they can, but none of them reaches the northernmost part of the monarchs' summer range.

The new generations of monarchs hatch into caterpillars in about four days, and after about two weeks of heavy feeding on milkweed, they pupate. One to two weeks later they emerge from their chrysalides ready to mate and continue north. Successive generations leapfrog northward, following the emergence of milkweed, until they reach Canada sometime in June.

The first monarchs we see in the North during the early summer represent a generation born en route from Mexico. More generations are born here, and we see lots of these handsome butterflies during the late months of summer. In fall, the youngest monarchs congregate and set out on the long flight back to Mexico. The mystery—and the miracle—of the monarch is how an animal as fragile and ethereal as a butterfly could have evolved such an awesome, long-distance flight as its most efficient way of surviving winter.

# POISON IVY
## *Learning to Look at Leaves*

*P*oison ivy is a problem for many people during the summer, but fall is actually a more dangerous time for those who have not yet learned to identify it. The brilliant red of its autumn leaves might tempt someone to pick a few for a leaf collection. And a bonfire of fall leaves, which could easily include some poison ivy, could spread fine droplets of irritating oil in sweet-smelling smoke.

Poison ivy varies so much in appearance and growth habits that a single picture or description of it can be deceiving. The best way to learn about poison ivy is to have someone who already knows it lead you to a patch so you can examine it closely in the wild.

One thing you will notice immediately is the pattern of

threes. Poison ivy belongs to a group of plants that have what are called compound leaves. When botanists classify plants, they describe leaves as either *simple* or *compound.* Simple leaves are like those of oaks and maples—one leaf grows at the end of each leaf stem. Compound leaves are either like a feather or like the fingers on your hand—several leaflets grow from a single leaf stem. Poison ivy's leaflets grow in threes at the end of each relatively short stem.

With your attention focused on one set of three leaflets, look for other identifying details. Each leaflet, for instance, has a smooth edge except for a notch or a few jagged teeth that seem to be placed randomly on the different leaflets. Also, each leaflet is slightly asymmetrical, the midrib dividing it into two not-quite-equal halves. Finally, the central leaflet is set apart from its two attendants by a short length of stem.

In addition to having variable leaves, poison ivy has variable growth habits. It can grow as a small woody plant, as a shrub, or as a vine that climbs up fenceposts and trees. Whereas many vines climb by twining, poison ivy vines produce little rootlets that penetrate cracks and hold on. These rootlets don't absorb nutrients, but they help the vine grow by absorbing water.

When you've examined enough poison ivy, you will recognize not only its identifying characteristics but its many variations. Knowing where poison ivy grows can also help you spot and avoid it. It loves the edges of pastures and parks, where it mixes into hedgerows and brush. It also likes open woods, beaches, sunny river banks, roadsides, the edges of railroad tracks, and even islands. Poison ivy is so widespread because over sixty species of birds eat the plant's white berries and deposit the undigested seeds with their droppings.

Every part of every poison ivy plant in every season contains poisonous oil, but not every person who touches the plant reacts to it in the same way. Some people are apparently immune, but immunity is not necessarily a permanent or absolute condition. Changes in diet or blood chemistry can change your reaction to the oil. Your sensitivity can also vary with the amount of sun, wind, or salt water your skin has been exposed to. Although you might tolerate a small amount of the oil, larger amounts might do you in.

Susceptible people develop the poison ivy rash only from direct contact with the oil, which does not always require direct contact with the plant. If you walk through a bed of poison ivy and get it on your shoes, you might transfer it to your hands when you take your shoes off. Pets are also great carriers. They can get the oil on their fur and innocently rub it onto your hands, arms, or face. In short, the oil does not float from a nearby poison ivy plant onto your skin, but it can travel by unexpected means, creating the illusion that you got it just by looking.

Poison ivy is one of those common, abundant things that everyone should learn to identify and understand in self-defense.

# CANADA GEESE
## *Learning to Observe Bird Behavior*

$O$ne of the clearest signs of fall is the sound of geese honking noisily overhead. If you keep your eyes trained on the part of the sky the honking is coming from, shortly you will perceive faint, almost invisible dots. These dots are usually arranged in a V-formation, or sometimes in a looser, undulating U.

Both the flight formation and the honking are important to the geese. Flying in a V allows the strongest individuals to break way while the rest of the flock follows along, each bird in the wake of the bird just in front of it. The honking is the flock's way of staying in touch. The leader honks a signal to follow, and the followers honk back that they are indeed following.

The commonest North American goose is the Canada goose, which nests in Canada and the northern United States and winters in the southern states. It is a large, brown-bodied bird with a black head and neck and a noticeable white patch that looks like a chin strap. The fall migrants we hear and see overhead have finished their northern nesting and are flying southward toward bodies of water that will stay open all winter. Although the nesting season is over, family groups have not broken up. A migrating flock usually consists of several families traveling together.

Family life is more persistent among geese than among most other birds. The young will remain with their parents through their first winter and will fly north with them again in the spring. Only when the parents begin nesting will the yearling geese gather together and move away. They must wait two more years before they will be ready to mate and raise families of their own.

Canada geese mate for life, and both parents play crucial roles in raising the young. The female, called the goose, builds a casual ground nest out of materials she finds close to her nesting site and lines it with down from her own breast. Because she is a ground nester, she and her five to six eggs make easy prey. The male, called the gander, stands guard and will fight fiercely in defense of his mate and eggs. The female does all the incubating, which takes about a month, but the male is always close by.

Young geese are *precocial* birds. They hatch from their eggs covered with down, and within twenty-four hours they are ready to leave the nest, never to return. The parents, however, must spend several more weeks protecting them and teaching them how to survive. The adult geese lead their downy goslings to water, where they help them find food and signal them when to dive to avoid danger. Because the adults molt after they've nested and lose all their flight feathers at once, they are as flightless as their young for about half of this learning-and-growing period. The parents are ready to fly again at about the same time that their young are learning to fly for the first time.

Canada geese spend more time out of water than other waterfowl do. They walk gracefully on dry land and frequently graze in fields close to water. Their preferred foods include sprouting grains, wild rice, sedges, marsh grasses, and other aquatic vegetation. They like the roots, shoots, leaves, and seeds of the plants they eat. They also eat aquatic insects, their larvae, and other small aquatic animals. In the fall, geese often graze the stubble of mowed fields for roots and fallen grain.

Flocks of geese, whether grazing or migrating, enjoy strong social bonds. Sentinels stand guard while the flock feeds, and senior geese take turns leading when the flock is in flight. Traditionally, a flock of migrating geese is supposed to tempt us to wander, but it should just as much encourage us to stay home.

# MALLARDS
## Learning to Understand Differences in Bird Behavior

*L*ike geese, ducks migrate in the fall, but they don't quack in flight to draw attention to themselves. You can see them best if you approach them by canoe. If you paddle around the marshy edges of ponds or lakes along the ducks' flyways, you will see thousands of them assembling to fly southward or resting along the way. The most familiar North American duck is the mallard.

Mallards have had a long and close association with human beings. Wild mallards were captured and domesticated as far back as the first century A.D., and the ease with which they accommodated themselves to captivity made them the ancestors of most of today's barnyard ducks. Mallards also nest by choice in city parks, which gives city dwellers a chance to observe the handsome green-headed males and the drabber, quacking females.

The mallard's Latin name, *Anas platyrhynchos*, describes one of its most noticeable features. *Anas* means simply "duck," *platy* means "broad," and *rhynchos* means "nose" or "beak." The mallard's broad beak is designed for scooping up aquatic vegetation on the surface of a pond and for breaking off or pulling up plants that grow in the water. Mallards feed mostly in shallow water, occasionally upending themselves to dunk for something, but only rarely diving beneath the surface for food. This manner of feeding groups them with other shallow-water feeders, who are referred to informally as "dabbling ducks."

Dabbling ducks spend most of their time paddling, dunking, and waddling along muddy shorelines. The position of their legs and the general arrangement of their body weight enables them to shift instantly from swimming to flying with just a few powerful wingbeats. Ducks that dive for their food, called "diving ducks," have their legs set farther back and their weight distributed for headfirst plunges into deep water. They must patter across the water's surface to gain some momentum before they can fly. If you paddle your canoe quietly toward a flock of mallards, you'll see how efficiently they take off. One second they're swimming serenely, and the next they're in full flight, their rapid wingbeats carrying them speedily into the distance.

Mallards differ significantly from Canada geese in their mating, nesting, and family life. The male mallard, called a drake, mates with the female, called a duck, for just one season and stays with her only until she has finished laying her eight to ten eggs. Then, unlike a gander, he's off with other males to molt into his drab eclipse plumage.

While the male is working his way through two molts, one to lose his bright colors and one to gain them back again, the female incubates her eggs for about a month and then cares alone for her growing young. Ducklings, like goslings, are precocial, so as soon as their down dries after hatching the solitary mother leads them to water. There she teaches them how to catch aquatic insects and how to stay close to her for protection. During this time she molts just once and loses her ability to fly. Although the flightless mother defends her small ducklings bravely, she might lose half of her brood to predators, storms, and other natural causes.

By fall the surviving young can fly, the females have regrown their flight feathers, and the males are handsome again in their new plumage. Soon all the mallards will join with other members of their species and with other ducks to participate numerously—but quietly—in the dramatic fall migration.

# PAINTED TURTLES
## *Learning to Observe a Turtle—I*

*A* marshy area full of ducks is also likely to be the home of painted turtles. Painted turtles are well named because they look as if they have been painted by an artist who specializes in reds and yellows. The upper shell, called the *carapace*, is edged with a red pattern resembling an American Indian motif. The dark surface of the shell itself is divided into sections by lines of pale yellow. The lower shell, called the *plastron*, is a bright yellow-orange.

The artist added more reds and yellows in the form of stripes on the turtle's head, then splashed two yellow spots right behind each eye. As a final touch, there are red streaks for the front legs and red speckles for the hind. The turtles seen in the East are called eastern painted turtles, but three other subspecies—the midland, southern, and western—inhabit other parts of North America. Each subspecies has its own distinctive pattern of reds and yellows.

Painted turtles are creatures of shallow fresh waters with muddy bottoms and lots of vegetation. They inhabit marshes, ponds, and lazy rivers, where rocks or fallen trees protrude from the water. They use these rocks and trees to sun themselves twice each day—once in the morning and again in the afternoon. Sometimes the turtles line up by the dozen, merging invisibly with the dark background until something disturbs them. Then there's a sudden scramble as they all slip into the water at once.

In addition to basking at regular times, painted turtles also eat at regular times. They forage during the late morning and again in the late afternoon. They are basically omnivorous, eating algae, aquatic plants, insects, crayfish, and snails. Because they eat both live and dead food, they serve as scavengers wherever they live. Hatchlings and young turtles eat more animal food in order to grow fast, while adults feed more on vegetable matter.

Painted turtles feed in water and always stay close to it. At night they sink to the bottom to sleep, and in winter they burrow deep into the soft underwater mud to hibernate during the coldest weather. Only the females ever leave the safety of the aquatic habitat. In early summer, when they are ready to lay their eggs, they crawl onto dry land, dig a nest with their hind feet, and deposit their two to twenty eggs.

The female does nothing for her offspring besides lay and bury the eggs, and perhaps lay and bury a second clutch a few weeks later. If the nest is not pillaged by a raccoon, skunk, or other predator, the hatchlings emerge from their eggs in about ten to eleven weeks. Their sex is dependent on the temperature of the nest during the middle third of the eggs' development. Nests with fluctuating or intermediate temperatures tend to produce approximately equal numbers of males and females, whereas warmer nests produce all females and cooler nests produce all males. Laboratory experiments have determined that the threshold temperatures are 88° F (31° C) or higher for all females and 77° F (25° C) or lower for all males. Unusually high or low temperatures may therefore produce a temporary excess of one sex or the other.

The hatchlings are so small that they are quite vulnerable for the first few months of their lives. They might be eaten by raccoons or snakes on their way from the nest to water, or by bullfrogs, large fish, or even other turtles when they reach the water. Some hatchlings stay in their underground nests through their first winter and emerge in the spring, when they can dash for water, feed on abundantly available food, and grow fast.

Despite predation of their eggs, variable sex ratios, and high hatchling mortality, painted turtle populations are fairly stable. And over the years they achieve an even mix between males and females. Because these turtles don't mate until they are five to seven years old, and because many individuals are still reproducing when they are over thirty, the generations of turtles appear slowly but steadily, with plenty of time to compensate for yearly variations.

# ACORNS
## Learning to Observe
## Ecological Relationships

$F$all means seeds, and one seed that means many things to many creatures is the acorn. Acorns are, of course, the seeds of oak trees, produced after the oak's small flowers, which bloom early in the spring, have been pollinated by the wind. Oak trees grow separate male and female flowers on the same tree, but only the female flower is evident in the mature acorn. The cap is an enlarged and stiffened version of the extremely small, overlapping leaves that protected the female flower before it blossomed. The acorn itself is the flower's ovary, grown large and hardened into a protective shell around the single seed within.

The seed, or nut, is highly nutritious and serves as an important food for many animals. To a certain kind of insect the acorn means not just food but a home. The snout beetle, also known as the acorn weevil, lays its eggs inside acorns. When the eggs hatch, the growing young eat the nut and live quite happily inside the shell until they are ready to emerge as adults. Some animals recognize acorns that are inhabited by these insects and actually prefer them. A shell full of insects might contain less nut meat, but it offers enough insect protein to compensate.

For some birds, such as ruffed grouse, wild turkeys, and wood ducks, the acorn is a staple food. These species have powerful gizzards that enable them to swallow acorns whole and grind them into digestible food. Some songbirds, such as blue jays and nuthatches, eat acorns too, but they peck through the hard outer shell and eat just the tender nut they find inside.

Human beings aren't big acorn eaters anymore, but American Indians in both the East and West once consumed them in great quantities. Different tribes developed different methods for leaching out the bitterness. Some buried them in wet ground, and others soaked them in streams until most of the tannic acid was gone. Then they either roasted the nuts or ground them into meal for bread or mush. Acorns were important to the Indians' winter diet because they could be harvested in abundance during the fall and easily stored for winter meals.

Many wild mammals also eat acorns, and some serve as the oak trees' agents in planting their seeds. Black bears and raccoons feast on acorns in the fall, while deer eat them in the fall and dig through snow for them during the winter. These animals, like the snout beetles and birds, play no role in planting new oak trees. But mice, chipmunks, and squirrels store acorns for winter food and sometimes inadvertently plant an oak tree by neglecting to eat one of their stored seeds.

Gray squirrels, with their particular method of storing acorns, are the oak trees' best agents. A gray squirrel at work looks as if it had been trained to plant trees. It carries each seed fifty to a hundred feet from the parent tree, scratches a shallow hole with its forefeet, deposits the seed, and covers it with soil and leaf litter. This shallow burial hides the seed from other animals, and if the gray squirrels themselves happen to miss it in their random searches for winter food, it is planted at the ideal depth for germination.

Whereas eaten acorns mean survival to many animals, planted acorns mean survival to the oaks—which means, of course, more acorns. This mutually perpetuating relationship between oak trees, acorns, animals, and new oak trees is just one of the many carefully worked out interdependencies that surround us in the natural world.

# GRAY SQUIRRELS
## *Learning to Observe Seasonal Behavior of Mammals*

Gray squirrels, because they depend on acorns and nuts for winter food, formerly inhabited the oak-hickory-beech forests that once covered much of eastern North America. When human settlers eliminated large tracts of this forest, some of these resourceful rodents learned to make do with city parks, cemeteries, and suburban yards, where landscapers left oaks and other nut trees for their beauty. Because gray squirrels share human habitats, it's easy to observe them and their seasonal behavior.

In the fall, two things are happening within gray squirrel communities: many of the young are leaving their home territories to search for new places to live, and the individuals who remain become busy storing winter food. The two phenomena are related. The number of squirrels who can live in any one area is limited by the amount of available food. Gray squirrels regulate their populations by driving out the young for whom there will not be enough to eat.

Many of the extras disperse in the fall, with a few more leaving in the spring. Most years these dispersals occur imperceptibly, the only evidence being solitary squirrels dashing through neighborhoods where they are not seen at other times of year. But some years gray squirrels seem to erupt, thousands of them traveling together in long-distance movements researchers call *mass migrations.* Because these mass migrations always occur in the fall and involve mostly young squirrels, they are probably related to the regular fall dispersals, but the researchers have not yet determined the exact causes of these larger movements, nor can they predict them.

The older squirrels and the younger ones who are permitted to stay to keep the local population stable spend the fall and winter relatively peacefully in their home ranges. Members of the local group recognize and tolerate each other but drive strangers out. During the fall, both young and old are busy foraging for acorns and other nuts and burying them individually around their home range for winter food. They don't really cooperate in this effort, but come winter they will eat each other's cached food as they find it. Random searching amidst the leaf litter and later under the snow will bring them close enough to smell a morsel of food, and at that time of year it's first come, first served. Because there are as many gray squirrels eating the buried nuts and acorns as there were burying them, most of these tree seeds are retrieved, but some few are always left. These seeds, if they germinate and grow into mature trees, are not lost—they will provide food for future generations of gray squirrels.

For several weeks in January and February, and again in June and July, gray squirrels live in a carnival atmosphere. These are their mating seasons. When a female is almost ready to mate, she begins attracting males—at first just a few, then more and more from greater distances, until she finds herself pursued by five to a dozen competitive suitors. At the outset she races away from them, and the males chase her and challenge each other, establishing a dominance hierarchy that will determine which male will mate with the female when she's ready.

One of the older males generally wins, but sometimes two

or three of almost equal age jockey for dominance right up to the moment the female becomes receptive. The male who happens to be at the front of the line at that moment mates with her and then defends her from the approaches of all the others. Eventually all the males—including the successful one—lose interest in the mated female and return to their home ranges until the noise of another mating chase brings them running again. The noise is important because it attracts unrelated males from distant ranges, which helps prevent inbreeding.

Gray squirrels who gather in great numbers in parks and around bird feeders are sometimes perceived as pests, but these resourceful natives are merely responding to concentrations of food that we've created. If you watch them closely throughout the year, you will see that they are less concerned with pestering us than they are with perpetuating their own species.

# FALL FOLIAGE
## Learning to Observe Changing Colors

*W*hile animals prepare for winter by hibernating, migrating, or storing food, trees prepare by shedding their leaves. But first the leaves turn colors. Sentimental pictures of Jack Frost with a paintbrush imply that fall colors are caused by the frost, but a frost that came before the colors would in fact prevent them. The whole process begins way back in June, but nothing shows until fall.

When a tree feels the days shortening after the summer solstice on June 21, it begins to change its relationship to its leaves. During spring and early summer the tree had been providing the leaves with plenty of minerals and fluids to support their food-manufacturing processes. But around midsummer it begins to pull its resources back in. It gradually deprives the leaves of their life-support system and finally abandons them altogether.

If you look closely at a leaf that is just beginning to show color, you will see advanced signs of this changing relationship between the tree and its leaves. A dying leaf is at first part green and part yellow. The green is *chlorophyll*, which was necessary to the leaf's food production, but which begins to break down at the end of the growing season. The yellow is caused by pigments called *carotenoids* and *xanthophylls*, the same pigments that color carrots, egg yolks, cream, and butter. These substances were present in the leaf all summer, but they were masked by the dominant green of the abundant chlorophyll. When the chlorophyll disappears, however, the underlying yellow becomes the dominant color.

The color changes in many species of trees stop here. Birches, aspens, poplars, and hickories contribute shades of yellow to fall's array of colors. But other trees produce new pigments in response to continuing changes within their leaves. The reds of maples, sumacs, and some oaks are caused by a pigment called *anthocyanin*, which also makes geraniums and apples their different shades of red. Anthocyanin forms in the cell sap of the dying leaves. The more sugar in the cell sap, the more brilliant the red. Likewise, the more acid, the more red.

Two other colors related to anthocyanin contribute to the richness and variety of fall foliage. Purples indicate anthocyanin in an alkaline cell sap, and flaming oranges form as the emerging reds mix with the underlying yellows. Because anthocyanin responds to light by becoming yet more brilliant, clear fall days invite trees to achieve their peaks of color before they finally shed their leaves for winter.

Although the browns of late fall are not as spectacular as the yellows, reds, purples, and oranges of Indian summer, they too tell us something about what the leaves are going through. As chemical changes continue in the dying leaf, the pigments oxidize, turning leaves brown just as a cut apple turns brown when exposed to air.

By the time leaves fall to the ground, they have undergone a number of chemical changes, but they're not finished yet. They are dead, but they still contain minerals and organic compounds. Worms, insects, and other organisms will feed on some of these substances, and water will leach others deep into the soil. Finally, one last color change will occur, unobserved and unobservable. The decomposing leaves will disappear as leaves, contributing the last of their shapes and colors to the rich dark humus that supports all forest life.

# AMERICAN ELM
## Learning to Understand the Impact of Humans—I

*A* dead elm is a sad sight. While other trees will grow their leaves again each spring, the elms will gradually become weathered skeletons, their branches strewn on the ground beneath them or amputated before they fall.

The story of the American elm offers a lesson in international ecology. This tall and handsome species was native to eastern North America and responded well to the arrival of European settlers. It wasn't useful for ship masts, nor did it lend itself to construction, so it wasn't harvested wholesale during the early centuries of our presence. The wood was used for furniture veneer, barrel staves, planks, railroad ties, and firewood, but the tree's major contribution was as a shade tree.

The American elm makes an excellent shade tree because of the way it grows. The trunk divides at a height of anywhere from ten to twenty feet; the branches grow upward for some feet, then arch and hang their twigs and leaves delicately downward. The mature tree looks like a vase holding a thick spray of flowers. Many settlers chose to have an elm near their houses to provide a broad circle of shade under a high and graceful canopy. Farmers left a few in their pastures and fencerows to provide shade for their livestock. Some communities decided to plant elms in their parks or even to line entire streets with them because the branches created natural archways.

By the early twentieth century, the American elm was firmly established as a favorite shade tree, but in the late 1920s a shipment of diseased elm logs was imported from Europe, and everything began to change. European elms were already suffering from a fungus disease that may have traveled from Asia to Europe during World War I. Because the disease was first detected in the Netherlands, it was named the "Dutch elm disease."

Once the Dutch elm fungus arrived in the United States, it didn't have much difficulty spreading itself. Elm bark beetles, both our native species and the European species that was imported with the diseased logs, carried fungus spores from the logs to healthy trees and then from diseased trees to other healthy trees. These beetles are called bark beetles because they spend the early part of their lives under the bark of dead or dying trees, where they tunnel, feed, and become covered with fungus spores. When they mature they fly to healthy elms, the European bark beetle to feed in the crotches of small twigs and the native bark beetle to feed on trunks and branches. They both deposit fungus spores wherever they go.

Once delivered by the insects, the spores enter the elm's conducting system and travel gradually throughout the tree. Colonies of the fungus clog the tree's vessels, cutting off the flow of water and nutrients to one group of leaves at a time. Eventually the whole conducting system becomes clogged, and the tree dies.

When the bark beetles are ready to lay their eggs, they leave the tree they have just infected and seek out dead or dying trees again. This cyclic relationship between elms and elm bark beetles keeps the disease spreading, and it might eventually kill all our elms. Foresters have been working hard to find a cure, but so far they haven't found a workable one.

During the summer you can still see the green leaves of surviving elms. And in the fall and winter you might notice an oriole's nest hanging from the tip of a naked branch—a sign that birds have raised their young amidst protective foliage within recent history. But if you keep count, you will find yourself confronted by far too many dead elms—big ones that must have been magnificent before the Dutch elm disease hit. It's sobering to think that if those diseased logs had never been imported, we'd still have our healthy native elms instead of the lonely skeletons that haunt our present landscapes.

# BARK BEETLES
## Learning to Interpret Insect Engravings

*I*f you examine some dead elm branches that have fallen to the ground or that you're about to burn to protect the other elms in your neighborhood, you are likely to see the distinctive marks left by the European or American elm bark beetles. Bark beetles are also called engraver beetles because they produce little patterns that look like engravings as they feed and grow under the tree's bark. Each species of bark beetle creates a different pattern, and the pattern reflects the nature of its family life.

Some of these beetles are monogamous, whereas others are polygamous. A monogamous female bark beetle bores through the tree's bark and emits a scent that attracts a male. She mates, and when she's ready to lay her eggs, she excavates a single gallery with little egg niches on either side, one for each egg.

Both the European and American elm bark beetles are monogamous, but their engravings are easy to tell apart. The European female excavates her gallery vertically, following the wood's grain. When her eggs hatch, the larvae dig their feeding galleries at right angles to the maternal gallery, cutting across the wood's grain. The engraving this species leaves looks somewhat like a long-legged centipede crawling up the tree trunk. The American female, in contrast, digs her egg gallery horizontally, across the wood's grain, while her larvae, digging at right angles, excavate with the grain. The resulting pattern also resembles a centipede, but this one is crawling around—rather than up—the elm tree.

As you continue to examine fallen branches and firewood, you'll notice the engravings of other species, too. Each species of beetle, in addition to producing a characteristic engraving, chooses certain species of trees. While elm bark beetles attack elms, Ips engraver beetles attack pines and spruces. The Ips males are polygamous, so the engravings this group leaves are entirely different from the engravings of the elm bark beetles.

The mature Ips male bores through the outer bark of his host evergreen and excavates a small nuptial chamber where he will receive his females. As he feeds on the tree, chemicals in his body mix with chemicals from the tree, and he emits a scent that is attractive to females of his species. He mates with them as they arrive.

Each female then bores her own tunnel, or egg gallery, in a different direction from the central nuptial chamber, so the engraving has three, four, or five radiating legs. The females deposit their eggs in individual niches spaced along the sides of the egg galleries, and when the larvae hatch, each one eats its own tunnel to make the engraving yet more complex and elaborate. Once the larva has grown to full size, it stops eating and pupates. When it emerges from pupation, the new adult bores its way through the outer bark to begin its search for a new host tree.

The work of bark beetles can be injurious to their hosts because both adults and larvae feed on the tree's living inner bark and, sometimes, on the sapwood. If enough individuals feed on one tree, they can girdle the inner bark, thereby killing the tree. Their entrance and exit holes also invite the invasion of fungi, and some species, such as the elm bark beetles, even carry the spores.

The only consolation in this insect-tree interaction is that many species of bark beetles prefer trees that are weak or dying anyway. If you learn to identify your local engravings, you will at least know what species of unseen beetles are quietly at work among your trees.

# LATE FALL
## TO CHRISTMAS

# PHRAGMITES
## *Learning to Observe Reeds and Grasses*

*A*s the colors and activities of fall give way to winter, the landscapes that wait to be covered by snow are somewhat barren. But at this time of year one tall plant is at its most attractive. It stands a full two or three feet above other dry weeds, and its feathery top waves in the wind like a cheerleader's pompon. These graceful plants with the pompon tops are called *Phragmites.*

*Phragmites* are aquatic grasses. They are also called reeds. Near coasts, these reeds find plenty of the wet soil they need and sometimes cover vast areas, but inland they tend to grow in smaller clumps beside roads, in median strips, along ditches, and near rivers. They usually grow in pure thick stands.

If you try to pick one of these attractive reeds for an indoor decoration, you will learn something about its growth habits. First, you can pull as hard as you want, but the plant will not come up by its roots. Actually, the roots are not what's holding it. Reeds spread by means of horizontal underground stems called *rhizomes*. Because rhizomes look like roots, they are often referred to as rootstocks. The reeds' rootstocks are thick, strong, and cling to the soil tenaciously—and the part of the plant you see aboveground is inseparably attached to them.

Because of their spreading rootstocks, reeds are excellent soil holders, protecting it from floods and other forces of erosion. But, also because of these rootstocks, reeds sometimes spread too far too fast. If you want to get rid of them, you can't just cut or plow them under like other weeds. You have to either dig up the rootstocks completely or drain the soil they're growing in to deprive them of the moisture they need.

If you still want the reed even though it won't pull easily out of the ground, you can try picking it like a flower. This effort will teach you something about the aboveground stalk. You will find that the stalk feels woody, like a chopstick, but it's hollow; and, instead of snapping like a chopstick, it splits and hangs on by stringy fibers. You could cut the frayed stalk with no difficulty with scissors or a knife, but if all you have are your hands, you'll need to bend, twist, and maybe even separate some of the fibers to break them individually. Finally, you'll have your decorative reed with its triumphant plume on top to help you forget about its slightly raggedy bottom.

The reed's stalk looks like a collapsible car antenna, with each section rising out of the one below it. The segments taper so the stalk becomes increasingly slender toward the top. This construction enables the tall plant to sway in the wind without breaking. The pompon on top is as attractive close up as it is from a distance. It consists of hundreds of fuzzy little seeds. Although these seeds are well equipped to fly, they don't leave willingly. Even if you run your hand over them, only a few seeds will come loose. Most of them are imperfect anyway and therefore not capable of producing new plants. Reeds spread more effectively by means of their persistent underground rootstocks.

Reeds play an important role in the orderly progression of events by which watery areas become dry land. Along with bulrushes and cattails, they fill in the edges of lakes, ponds, rivers, and estuaries, gradually trapping enough soil to create environments suitable for other kinds of plants. Once they've created a habitat too dry for themselves, they die out and plants that thrive in drier soils replace them.

Many botanists disdain phragmites because they are imported plants and because they sometimes displace native vegetation, but these roadside, riverside reeds make a special contribution to late fall scenery. The grace with which they bend and sway in the chilling winds lends beauty to this barren time of year.

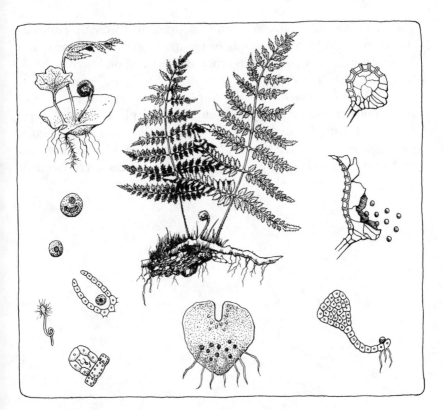

# FERNS

## Learning to Observe the
## Uniqueness of Ferns

*A* small group of plants that show to their best advantage during the colorless weeks between leaf drop and the first snow are the evergreen ferns. Most ferns turn brown and brittle with fall frosts, but three common woodland species stay green all winter. By learning to tell the evergreen species apart, you can introduce yourself to the basics of fern identification. But first, what is a fern?

Ferns are green plants, which differentiates them from mushrooms, but they don't flower or produce seeds, which differentiates them from trees and flowering plants. They are modern in that they have roots, stems, leaves, and internal vessels to transport fluids, but they are also primitive in that they reproduce by means of spores. Ferns occupy a position on the evolutionary ladder somewhere between primitive plants, which are still dependent on water for some phases of their life cycles, and modern plants, which have become completely adapted to life on dry land.

The ferns we see in temperate regions today are much smaller than their ancestors. During the warm Carboniferous Period, about 240 million years ago, ferns grew like trees, with thick round trunks supporting a crown of huge fronds. Some tree ferns still persist in the tropics, but most species adapted to the cooling climate that followed the Carboniferous by becoming smaller and hiding their trunks underground as thick horizontal structures called rhizomes, or rootstocks.

A fern's reproductive strategy requires that it pass through two generations before producing a new fern. Botanists call this two-part life cycle an *alternation of generations.* One generation begins when the mature fern produces millions of spores in little spore cases that grow on the undersides of its leaves. Unlike a seed, which holds a miniature plant inside its protective covering, a spore is a single cell which, if it lands on suitable soil, can divide and become more cells. A germinating fern spore grows into a strange little plant that doesn't look at all like a fern. This plant, which is called a *prothallus,* is rarely noticed by anyone except the most dedicated botanists. It's green, heart-shaped, about the size of your little fingernail, and it lives only long enough to produce the next generation—the familiar fern.

The underside of the prothallus produces both male and female organs. It is at this stage of the fern's life cycle that it is still dependent on water. A sperm must swim through a thin film of moisture—a dewdrop, a raindrop, or spray from a splashing brook—to the female organ and fertilize the egg waiting inside. The fertilized egg grows into a tiny fern, feeding on the nutrients in the prothallus until it establishes its own roots and leaves. Several months or years later, when the mature fern produces its own spores, the two-phase life cycle is complete.

Ferns are perennial, so the established plant produces new fronds every year. The way the new fronds unfurl differentiates ferns from other lacy-looking green plants that you might think are ferns. If you poke around toward the center of a clump of evergreen ferns in the fall, you will feel the tops of several hard, round structures. These are next year's fronds, already formed but coiled tightly against the rootstock. Come spring, these tight little coils will unroll, looking for a while like fiddleheads, then expanding into full and graceful fronds. Other green plants grow straight upward, led by their growing tips. Once you can distinguish a fern from other plants, you're ready to begin distinguishing the different ferns from each other.

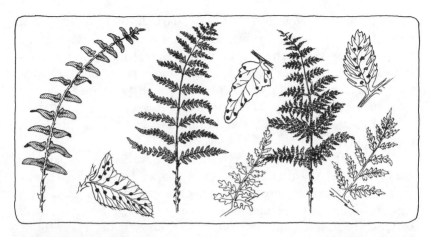

# EVERGREEN FERNS
## *Learning to Observe Differences in Ferns*

*I*f, when you first address yourself to ferns, you limit yourself to the evergreen species, you will find fern identification quite manageable. The three commonest evergreens—the Christmas fern, the marginal woodfern, and the spinulose woodfern—grow in rocky, hilly woods and are frequently found close together.

The evergreen ferns you see in the fall woods have already shed their millions of spores, but one way to tell the three species apart is to examine the old spore cases on the undersides of their fronds. These spore cases look like little dots—they are, in fact, called *fruitdots*—and each species has its own characteristic arrangement.

The Christmas fern is a large, dark, leathery-looking fern with its fruitdots located on shriveled leaflets at the tops of its fertile fronds. When the fruitdots were new, they were arranged in neat rows, but later they expanded and merged until, by fall, they look like solid, cinnamon-colored fuzz. If you look at a leaflet that hasn't shriveled, you'll notice it resembles a miniature Christmas stocking, which should help you remember this fern's common name.

The two other evergreen ferns, both called woodferns, are closely related, but they can be distinguished by the relative laciness of their fronds and by the location of their fruitdots. Fern experts refer to degrees of laciness as *once-cut, twice-cut,* and *thrice-cut.* To understand these distinctions, you need to imagine each frond as a green leaf that has been cut with scissors to create the pattern that characterizes the species. A Christmas fern is once-cut; the scissors have cut once around each little Christmas stocking without making any additional cuts for decoration. Each individual Christmas stocking, because it is a subdivision of the leaf, is called a leaflet.

The marginal woodfern is lacier than the Christmas fern, but not as lacy as its evergreen cousin the spinulose woodfern. It is twice-cut: the scissors have made one set of cuts up both sides of the frond to create leaflets, then turned themselves ninety degrees to make a second set of cuts dividing each of the leaflets into subleaflets. If you look at the backs of several of these twice-cut fronds, you will find one that has little cinnamon-colored fruitdots on it. They grow close to the edges, or margins, of the small subleaflets, which explains the "marginal" in this fern's common name.

The spinulose woodfern, named for its spiny laciness, is much fancier in its cutting than the marginal woodfern. Because it's so lacy and stays green, florists frequently use it as a decorative background in their flower arrangements. The spinulose woodfern is thrice-cut: the scissors have made yet a third set of cuts on this one, dividing each of the subleaflets into exceedingly small lobes. If your eye isn't very good at distinguishing twice- and thrice-cutness, you can rely on the fruitdots to tell a spinulose from a marginal woodfern. The little dots on the back side of the fertile spinulose fronds are more centered than those on the marginal fronds.

Identifying ferns can become an obsession during spring and summer when all the green fronds of the many different species are unfurled, but during late fall, with only a few species of evergreens to distinguish, fern identification is a comfortably manageable task.

# CROWS
## Learning to Observe Adaptability in Birds

Certain images characterize the bleak time of year between fall foliage and the first snow. One is that of a flock of crows feeding in an empty cornfield. There's something about these coal-black birds pecking amidst the corn stubble that seems like a comment on human activities: "The growing season is over, you busy humans. Now survive winter if you can."

The crows will have no trouble surviving. Many of them fly south and roost together in huge flocks close to good feeding grounds. The crows that stay in the North congregate in smaller flocks around garbage dumps and farms, where they find plenty to eat among human leftovers.

Crows, in fact, find plenty to eat all year because they are opportunists. They eat what's available when it's available, and they have no difficulty shifting their diets to accommodate special circumstances. If it's a good year for grasshoppers, they will eat them by the hundreds, but if grasshopper populations are low, they will merely eat more beetles, grubs, caterpillars, and other ground-dwelling insects. Crows love corn and other human crops, but they also eat acorns, mulberries, wild cherries, and the seeds of sumac, poison ivy, Virginia creeper, and other wild plants. Crows eat birds' eggs and nestlings when they can get away with it, and they eat carrion—especially road kills—wherever they find it. In a study of the crow's diet, scientists identified 650 different food items in the stomachs of 2,118 crows gathered from around the United States and Canada.

Crows have prospered in the years since European settlers arrived on this continent, in large part because our foods have become their foods. Also, the clearing of land to plant food crops created the kind of mixed habitat crows prefer. They like trees for nesting near open fields for feeding. As human populations increased and spread westward, crows also increased their numbers and moved into areas such as the midwestern prairies, where they hadn't lived before. They are now common all over the United States except in the western deserts. Even our cities and suburbs appeal to them. These bold natives have been known to nest near the Pentagon and feed on the White House lawn.

In addition to being opportunistic eaters and bold nesters, crows are also smart. In the laboratory, for instance, they have learned to distinguish among circles, triangles, squares, and hexagons and to count as high as four. Both scientists and owners of pet crows (such ownership is now illegal) have commented on the crow's ability to learn from experience and to adapt to situations they've never experienced before. Crows seem to understand cars, guns, and other threats to their well-being more clearly than other animals do.

Furthermore, crows compound their individual advantages by sharing an interest in each other's welfare. When a flock is feeding, one crow acts as a sentinel, warning others with an alarm call if danger approaches. A different call rallies all the crows within hearing distance to mob an owl, hawk, or other predator. Researchers have determined that crows have a vocabulary of twenty-three different sounds, and to these bird sounds might be added their ability to imitate human words and laughter.

Crows aren't capable of verbalizing their thoughts about human beings, but as they feast in the corn stubble, they seem superior and indifferent. They have learned that wherever human beings congregate, there will be plenty of food for birds who are smart, alert, and not too picky about what they eat.

# RAVENS
## Learning to Observe
## Distinguishing Details

*R*avens look very much like crows, and from a distance it's easy to confuse them. But they are very different in size, flight, sound, and behavior. The best way to tell them apart is to watch the bird you're wondering about for as long as it will let you and then to analyze everything you've seen.

A raven is quite a bit bigger than a crow, which doesn't help at all if you're looking at a single black bird way off in the distance. Its body is twenty-two to twenty-seven inches long, while the crow's is only seventeen to twenty-one inches. A raven's wingspan is about four feet, while the crow's is closer to three. As befits its larger size, the raven's bill is heavier than the crow's, and it is curved strongly downward. Finally, given a close or magnified view, you can look at the bird's throat feathers for another distinguishing detail. A raven has long, pointed throat feathers that look like a rough beard, while the crow's throat is smooth.

If the bird you're watching flies, you'll have other clues to consider. For instance, the raven's spread tail is wedge-shaped, while the crow's is rounded. The two species also fly in different ways. The crow's typical flight pattern is a strong flap, flap, flap with occasional short glides. When gliding, it tilts its wings slightly upward. The raven spends more time gliding, or soaring, than flapping. It flaps a few beats and then soars for a while. When soaring, it holds its wings straight out. Crows fly to get somewhere, but ravens sometimes fly just for the fun of it, dropping, rolling, and sideslipping through air currents in an impressive display of aerial acrobatics.

All these visual details are helpful in telling the two species apart, but even more helpful are their characteristic sounds. The crow utters a familiar *caw, caw, caw,* whereas the raven's call is a hoarse croak that doesn't sound much like a bird. Other differences between these two closely related species are behavioral; to observe them you must pay attention not just to the birds but to their surroundings.

While crows responded to the arrival of European settlers by nesting close to human communities, ravens responded by withdrawing deeper into the wilderness. They prefer trees a considerable distance from civilization for their nesting—or, better yet, wilderness cliffs high up on mountains and along rocky coasts. So if your bird hangs around farm fields or the suburbs, it's probably a crow. If it's near the deep evergreen forests of the North, however, or high up on a mountain, or in the vicinity of isolated sea cliffs, it's more likely to be a raven.

While crows followed human beings westward, extending their range over most of the United States, ravens preceded the westward movement, seeking out what was left of the wilderness. Their range diminished, with very few of these shy and wary birds remaining in the East. Interestingly enough, ravens are not afraid of all human beings. They have learned to avoid the types that shoot at, trap, and poison them, but they're almost tame near Indian tribes that respect their presence as scavengers. But generally, ravens have found it more advantageous to keep company with wild animals. On Isle Royale in Michigan, where one of the last populations of timber wolves in the United States survives on a protected island, ravens follow the wolves on their hunts to enjoy the moose carrion that's left after the wolves have finished feeding. In the West, ravens follow coyotes much as they follow timber wolves in the North.

With just a glimpse of a large black bird from a distance, even experienced bird watchers have difficulty telling a raven from a crow. But if you get a close look at the bird and use habitat and behavior to help you, you should be able to figure out which of the two you're looking at.

# MISTLETOE
## Learning to Understand Plant
## Relationships

The Christmas season brings several plants right into our homes. It's the mythology that surrounds them that makes them popular indoor decorations, but each also has its own biology. Of all the Christmas plants, mistletoe has the most unusual habits.

The sprig of greenery you've just bought to hang over a doorway might not seem unusual, but if you think about it, two unusual features become evident: it's an evergreen with flat leaves instead of needles, and it's bearing fruit, little white berries, in the middle of winter. The mistletoe that's sold during the Christmas season has not been cultivated indoors to keep it green and fruiting. It has been harvested from the wild and arrives at your house just as it was growing in Texas, Oklahoma, or New Mexico a few weeks before Christmas.

In the South, where several species of broad-leaved trees stay green throughout the winter, mistletoe might not arouse much curiosity, but in the North, where all trees except the needled conifers shed their leaves in the fall, a clump of green growing on a barren branch would invite attention. While the common American mistletoe doesn't grow north of New Jersey and Pennsylvania, the European species that gave mistletoe its mythology grows in the cold northern areas that were home to the ancient Celts and Teutons. There it grows as a bushy evergreen on the leafless branches of apple trees, poplars, maples, and—rarely—oaks.

The Celts, whose priests were called druids, considered mistletoe sacred, especially if it happened to be growing on an oak. Finding this special mistletoe was always the occasion for a ritual harvest and feast. Ordinary mistletoe was honored too, but more routinely. Because it stayed green all winter, it was considered a place where woodland spirits might be hiding during cold weather. It was brought indoors to offer the spirits warmth and to decorate human homes with greenery during the long dark days of winter.

Whereas mistletoe's evergreen leaves won it honor and, eventually, commercial value, its sticky white berries win the species its future. These berries are attractive to several species of birds, who feed on them and transport them in one of two ways. Sometimes a berry sticks to the bird's beak, to be rubbed off on the branch of a tree when the bird stops to groom. In other cases, the bird eats a berry and deposits the undigested seed in its droppings on a branch beneath its perch.

If the seed is fortunate enough to land on a tree of the same species the parent plant grew on, it's ready to become a new mistletoe. The seed germinates and sends a modified root called a *haustorium* through the tree's bark and into its conducting tissues. Through this haustorium the mistletoe absorbs water and mineral salts. Its leaves contain chlorophyll, so the plant can manufacture its own food once the host tree has provided the necessary water and minerals.

Because mistletoe can manufacture its own food, it is only

a partial parasite, depending on its host only for what its own roots would provide if they grew in the soil. By growing high up in a tree, however, mistletoe gains the advantage of the tree's height—access to the sun—without having to support the tree's massive structure. The common Christmas mistletoe does not seriously damage the tree it grows on. Its strategy is to take only what it needs and to stay alive as long as its host.

Despite its parasitic habits, mistletoe has been a positive phenomenon in the cultures that have attached importance to it. It has been used in rituals for peace, fertility, safety in battle, good luck, good health, and protection against evil spirits. The custom of kissing under a sprig of mistletoe reflects these ancient associations and enhances the Christmas mood of open affection and general accord.

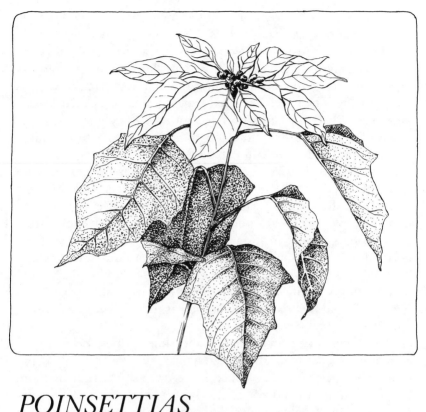

# POINSETTIAS
*Learning to Observe a Plant's Life Cycle*

*U*nlike mistletoe, which is harvested from the wild for the Christmas trade, poinsettias must be nurtured indoors under carefully controlled conditions. They are natives of Mexico and Central America, where they bloom naturally in winter. Our North American horticulturists have merely learned how to simulate the poinsettia's natural environment in order to produce these Christmas plants.

In the wild, poinsettias grow on rocky hillsides and the moist banks of ravines. They are tall and unkempt, not at all like the stunted and groomed plants we find in foil-covered pots at Christmas. But the flowers—or, more accurately, the leaves that surround the flowers—of both the wild and cultivated poinsettias are the same brilliant red, and they are what attracted attention to poinsettias in the first place.

If you look closely at a potted poinsettia, you will see the basic structure that characterizes this plant. At the center of the red leaves are clusters of very small yellowish-green flowers. They look more like waxen clubs than flowers, but everything needed for reproduction, including nectar for visiting insects, is located here. The specialized red leaves, which are called *bracts*, are not just there for Christmas decorations. They play an important biological role. It's their job to attract insects to the small flowers that need to be pollinated.

In 1828 the first United States minister to Mexico, who had an interest in botany as well as in diplomacy, brought some samples of the Mexican "flower of Christmas Eve" home with him. He lived in Charleston, South Carolina and could grow these tropical plants in his warm southern garden. When other horticulturists saw Joel Roberts Poinsett's beautiful flower, which became known in this country as the poinsettia, they began experimenting with it. They discovered that it would not grow in the North, and that day length as well as temperature was important to its annual cycle.

Eventually a Swiss immigrant named Albert Ecke discovered exactly what poinsettias need in order to flower at Christmas time. They need seventy consecutive days of thirteen or more hours of darkness at 60–65° F (15–18° C) before they will bloom. In Mexico and Central America the timing and temperatures are perfect, and poinsettias bloom quite naturally during the Christmas season. But in most of North America, we have to bring these sensitive plants indoors to protect them from our cold climate. We thus give them too much artificial light, disrupting their natural flowering cycle.

If you want your poinsettia to bloom again next Christmas in accordance with its natural life cycle, you will need to fertilize the plant, cut it back to just its woody stems, transplant it outdoors for the summer, and bring it back indoors in the fall. Then you will need to enforce a thirteen-hour night for seventy days before Christmas by covering your poinsettia with a box or paper bag when you turn on your lights after mid-October. Ecke also discovered that if a poinsettia is ready to bloom before Christmas, it can be slowed down by exposing it to an hour or two of light every night to interrupt the natural cycle.

When you consider how demanding it is to manage a

poinsettia in the North, you might decide it would be easier just to go to Mexico for Christmas. There you would see these colorful plants growing tall and wild on the hillsides—blooming right on schedule because their genes are telling them to.

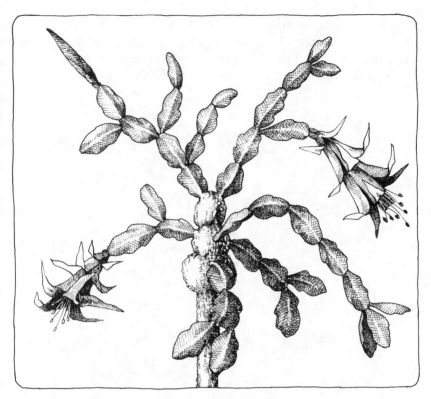

# CHRISTMAS CACTUS
## Learning to Observe a Cactus That Doesn't Grow in the Desert

The winter-blooming Christmas cactus, which many people keep as house plants throughout the year, comes from even farther away than the poinsettia. In the wild, it grows in the tropical forests of Brazil. It is a true cactus, with the water-retaining ability that marks the family, but it grows in a habitat very different from the habitat of the desert cacti and therefore grows in a completely different way.

Whereas the familiar desert cacti of the southwestern United States and Mexico grow directly out of the sandy desert soil, the Christmas cactus grows high up in a forest tree. It's an *epiphyte*—a plant that grows on another plant without being parasitic on it. An epiphyte derives its moisture and mineral nutrients from the air and sometimes, as in the case of the Christmas cactus, from the accumulated organic matter decaying in crotches of trees. An epiphyte in no way draws on the tree's resources. It uses the tree only to gain access to the filtered sunlight available near the top of the forest canopy.

The Christmas cactus and its close relative the Thanksgiving cactus, which is sometimes sold as a Christmas cactus, have become popular house plants in North America because they are relatively easy to care for. If properly managed, the Christmas cactus will produce its beautiful red flowers at Christmas time year after year. The Thanksgiving cactus, as its name implies, is more likely to flower in November. If it's important to you to have the Christmas-blooming species, look closely at the flat segments that constitute the stems and branches of both these cacti. The Christmas cactus, which goes by the Latin name *Schlumbergera bridgesii*, has smooth-edged, scalloped segments, while the Thanksgiving cactus, *Schlumbergera truncata*, has toothed segments with spines.

These segments, which look somewhat like a chain of flattened leaves, are actually flattened stem tissue. Like the desert cacti, the Christmas cactus has evolved a specialized stem that can perform the job of leaves—that is, make food—without sacrificing the water that typical leaves lose to the atmosphere. These stems can also swell to store water when it's available. Because water conservation and storage are essential to plants that live in dry climates such as the desert, or alternately wet and dry climates such as the tropics, the cacti and many other plants called *succulents* have developed impressive water-saving adaptations.

To invite your water-efficient Christmas cactus to flower at Christmas, you actually have to deprive it of water in the fall. In its native habitat, this cactus enjoys two dry periods during which it rests—one before it flowers and one after it flowers. It also experiences a period of short days and long nights during the time it's producing its flower buds. To simulate these Brazilian conditions in your home, you must slow down your watering in September, giving your plant just enough water to keep it from shriveling and allowing it to rest for six to eight weeks. If you have a room that doesn't get used after dark in the fall, you can station the resting plant there. Otherwise you'll have to cover it each evening to assure it at least thirteen hours of uninterrupted darkness. If you can't control the light your plant will be exposed to, perhaps you can manipulate the temperature. At a cool 50–55° F (10–13° C), the Christmas cactus will produce buds no matter how much light it gets.

After the six- to eight-week rest, the plant is ready for its wet season. The watering you give your Christmas cactus in mid-to-late October will encourage it to flower in December. Then, after it has added its red flowers to your Christmas decorations, it will need another six to eight weeks of rest before it's ready to be watered again for its spring and summer growing season. All in all, a Christmas cactus is easier to manage than a poinsettia, but you still must understand and respect its annual rhythms if you want it to perform for you each year at Christmas.

# CHRISTMAS TREES
## Learning to Identify Your Holiday Tree

*T*he Christmas tree has become such a prominent part of our American Christmas that it seems as if it has aways been with us. But the American Christmas tree is a relatively recent development. It wasn't until the 1850s that indoor evergreens became big business in this country. Before that they had been popular in Germany, parts of Europe, and communities where German immigrants had settled in the United States, but it took an entrepreneur living in the mountains of upstate New York to introduce Christmas trees to the nation.

The meaning of a Christmas tree is still the subject of scholarly debate, but its physical characteristics are less abstract. A Christmas tree is an evergreen tree either cut from the local woods or purchased from a local dealer which, carried indoors, becomes the bearer of all your Christmas ornaments. If you'd like to know what species of evergreen your Christmas tree happens to be, you can look at it as a forester would.

First, look at the needles to determine whether they are growing in groups, called *bundles,* or individually on the twigs. If your tree has longish needles growing in bundles, your tree is a pine. Scotch pine, with two needles per bundle, has become a national favorite, while white pine, with five needles per bundle, also has a following.

If your tree has short needles either growing flat against the twigs like scales or growing one by one the length of the twigs, you can apply some other tests. Scalelike foliage indicates one of the species called cedars. If the greenery looks feathery, as if it's been ironed flat, it's a white cedar. If it has some prickly needles sticking out beyond the scales, it's a red cedar. The cedars aren't as popular as some other evergreens marketed as Christmas trees, but if you cut your own tree, you might find yourself with one.

If you haven't identified your tree so far, you still have two popular short-needled groups left. At this point, it would be helpful to shake hands with your tree. If the needles are sharp to the touch, you have a spruce. Another way to check for a spruce is to roll a single needle between your finger and thumb. A spruce needle is four-sided and rolls easily. Popular Christmas tree species include black, white, red, blue, and Norway spruces.

If the needles on your tree are blunt, stiff—but not sharp—to the touch, and flat in cross section, chances are the tree is a fir, but modern Christmas-tree growers have confused evergreen identification by growing several different species called firs. The traditional Christmas fir is the balsam fir, which grows in the Northeast, the Great Lakes states, and Canada. A closely related southern fir, called the Fraser fir, is also marketed as a Christmas tree. Douglas fir, which is a western tree that resembles true firs but belongs to a different genus, has become very popular with Christmas-tree farmers and buyers all over the United States.

To tell a Douglas fir from a true fir, remove a needle and look at the mark that's left. If it is small and raised, you have a Douglas fir. If it's fairly large, round, and slightly depressed, you have one of the true firs. Look at the needle you've removed to double-check yourself. If the needle has a little stalk where it was connected to the twig, it's a Douglas fir. If the needle was connected directly to the twig and looks as if it has a little suction cup at its base, it's a true fir.

Each species of Christmas tree has its own native range and preferred growing conditions, but with Christmas-tree farmers growing nonnative trees and Christmas-tree sellers marketing the trees they can obtain most readily, you won't be able to learn where and how your particular tree grows in the wild until you learn its name.

# WINTER, MORE WINTER, AND WAITING

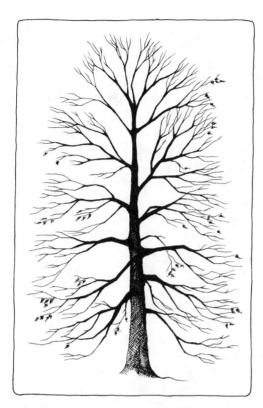
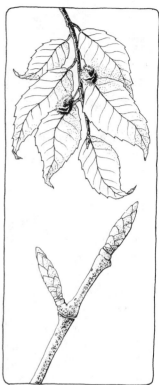

# BEECH TREES
## Learning to Observe the Anatomy of a Tree

*W*inter is a good time for tree study, and not just of evergreens. Evergreens may draw attention to themselves with their green needles, but the leaf-dropping, or *deciduous*, trees are worth looking at, too. You can see bark textures and twigs more clearly with the leaves gone, and you can observe the shapes and arrangements of winter buds. Beech is a likely tree to study first because its smooth gray bark makes it easy to spot from a distance.

Beech trees look like elephant legs. They grow straight and round, and their bark looks more like skin than bark. Actually, it is more like skin than the cracked and fissured coverings of other trees. While typical tree bark is a thick dead layer that splits as the living tree inside it grows in girth, beech bark is very thin. The living cells that produce it are close to the surface, and the dead, nongrowing outer layer is so thin that it sloughs off as powdery fragments rather than splitting into ridges and fissures.

Because beech has living tissue so close to its surface, it scars easily. Any tree that is gashed or injured deeply enough will produce protective scar tissue, called *wound cork*, but in most species the scar blends right into the rough outer bark. Beeches, in contrast, show even the slightest wounds—such as the claw marks of a bear who climbed the tree for its nutritious beechnuts. The scar tissue swells into raised bumps that outline and accentuate every injury. It has been the beech tree's misfortune to attract lovers' initials and other graffiti simply because its sensitive bark advertises such carvings with the cork it forms to heal its wounds.

You can also recognize a beech tree from a distance because of its tendency to hang onto some of its leaves through winter. Most deciduous trees completely separate themselves from their old leaves by forming a layer of wound cork—called an *abscission layer*—where the leaves had been attached. The leaves then fall of their own weight or are knocked off by rain and wind. Oaks and beeches don't form complete abscission layers, so some of their dead leaves hang on until next year's leaves push them off. Winter beech leaves are papery, light tan, and sound like wind chimes in gentle breezes. Oak leaves, in contrast, are thick, darker brown, and sound merely like rustling leaves.

While the smooth gray bark and persistent leaves will help you find a beech, its winter twigs will help you confirm your identification. Twigs are a tree's growing tips, and they are as different from species to species as leaves, flowers, and seeds are. Winter twigs have buds containing next year's leaves and flowers, and scars where last year's leaves fell away.

The most notable feature of a beech twig is its long pointed buds. They are set alternately and at sharp angles to the twig, which creates a zigzag look. Each bud is covered by tightly overlapping scales designed to protect the folded leaves and flowers all winter and to fall away in the spring. At the base of each bud—to the left or right of center—is the scar from last year's leaf.

Beech trees are a major component of eastern deciduous forests, but many of them have been cut as the forests have been cleared. Mature beeches still grow in parks, woodlots, and yards, however, where their bur-covered nuts provide food for wildlife. Winter is a good time to acquaint yourself with this familiar species and perhaps, by observing its bark and twigs, to cultivate an interest in other leafless trees.

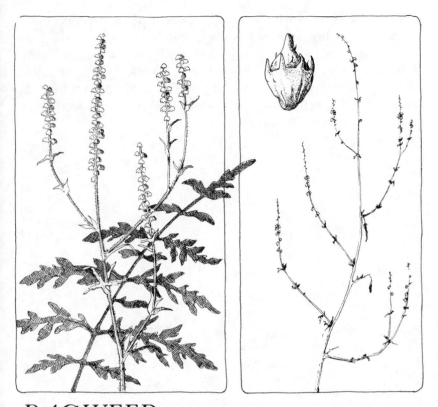

# RAGWEED
## Learning to Appreciate a Weed

*W*hile winter obliterates wild flowers, it leaves us winter weeds. And it transforms one of the most notorious from a nuisance into a lifesaver. Ragweed is a problem during late summer because its pollen causes "hay fever," but in winter many birds depend on its oil-rich seeds.

"Hay fever" is an inappropriate name for what ragweed does to some people because the allergy is caused by many things other than hay and it doesn't involve a fever. Basically, it's an allergy to pollen. Early-spring hay fever is a reaction to tree pollens. Summer hay fever is a reaction to grass pollens. Ragweed, which seems to get a disproportionate share of the blame, is responsible only for late-summer hay fever because that's the only time of year it produces pollen.

Many flowers are pollinated by insects, and their pollen doesn't cause the human species any inconvenience. It tends to be heavy and sticky—just the right consistency to be transported on the legs and bodies of insects. Also, there's not very much of it per flower. It's the wind-pollinated species, such as ragweed, that cause the problems.

During late summer, ragweed produces numerous greenish male flowers at the tops of tall stems, and each one produces great quantities of microscopic pollen. The wind blows this pollen into the atmosphere, where some of it lands on female ragweed flowers, which are hidden in the forks of upper branches and at the bases of the leaves. Much of this pollen never reaches female flowers, however, and is merely a free gift to the late-summer atmosphere.

Ragweed contributes to human allergy problems only during the late weeks of summer and affects only about five to ten percent of the population in the United States, but these same plants—the ones that manage to get their female flowers pollinated—offer food for wild birds during the most stressful time of year. Each ragweed produces many seeds, and some of them cling to the plants, which stand above snow throughout the winter. While the raggedy leaves that give ragweed its name have withered by the time the snow falls, the thin, branched stems, brittle as they are, withstand wind and weather to offer sparrows, finches, and other seed-eaters valuable winter meals.

With its mixed offerings, ragweed raises an ecological question. If we decided to exterminate it to help human beings who suffer from late-summer hay fever, we would be depriving many birds of a significant portion of their winter food. Which is more important: freedom from allergies or food for winter birds?

But perhaps this is one question ecologists won't have to answer. Ragweed is such a persistent and abundant plant that we couldn't exterminate it even if we tried. Its seeds have been known to remain viable for five years, and they germinate readily wherever they find a little exposed soil. Even if we could manage to eliminate it in one area, its pollen can travel for over a hundred miles, so we'd still have problems unless we could eliminate it nationwide.

It seems that the best we can do with our hardy native ragweeds is to cheer the winter birds who eat their seeds. Their appetites are the hay-fever sufferer's best ally.

# SNOW BUNTINGS
## Learning to Observe Winter Birds

*W*hen we think of birds migrating for winter, we think of them heading south, but for some arctic species the northern United States is south. Of these regular winter visitors, the snow bunting carries with it the most evidence of its northern preference. Its basic color is white, and it is completely at home in the snow.

Snow buntings arrive in the United States about the time the snow does. They are extremely gregarious at this time of year, sometimes traveling in groups of more than a thousand birds. Their winter diet consists mostly of weed seeds—including the seeds of ragweed—so they search out fields where weeds still stand above the snow. They are ground feeders and spend most of their waking hours walking or running about snowy fields in search of food.

Snow buntings have strong, sharp beaks to help them crack the hard-shelled seeds they find. Although they are related to the finches and sparrows who take seeds from bird feeders, you won't see snow buntings in your yard. They are strictly birds of open spaces—farm fields, airports, and beaches. Even at night they avoid trees. They find sheltered spots under tufts of grass and sleep in the same field they have been foraging in all day.

The snow buntings we see in the United States during winter are in their subdued winter plumage. The male has rusty-brown on his back, head, and wings. For his courtship, he will lose all the brown and turn a stark black and white. The female is similarly colored, but in winter she has more rusty-browns, and during the nesting season her whites remain tinged with rusty streaks.

Because of their coloration, snow buntings are difficult to see against the snow. Even if you don't get an opportunity to observe an individual, however, you might see a flock start up from a weedy field or perhaps land to feed. Their flocks seem to obey invisible commands. The birds wheel and turn in unison, seeming much more oriented to the group in their flying than they do in their scattered feeding.

Early in the spring, snow buntings head back north to nest in the relative privacy of the Arctic. While we down here watch for the arrival of our first robins, the residents of Alaska await their snow buntings with similar enthusiasm. The early males establish territories amidst rock piles or cliffs. The females arrive later, and then the pairing begins. After a male and female have chosen each other, the female searches the territory for a nook or cranny in which to build a sheltered nest. She does all the nest-building and incubating herself, but the male brings her food, and later, when the young have hatched, he helps feed them and keep the nest clean.

In addition to becoming territorial during the nesting season, snow buntings also change their diet. They shift from weed seeds to the abundantly available insects who are taking advantage of the brief arctic summer to reproduce. Adult snow buntings still eat some plant food, but they feed their young only insects, which offer more body-building protein.

Human beings who feel overwhelmed by northern winters should look to snow buntings and other arctic visitors to help them appreciate their environment. Some birds fly away to the sunny tropics, but others find the snowy North ideal.

# STARLINGS
## Learning to Understand the Impact of Humans—II

Starlings can be seen almost everywhere at any time of year. They are short-tailed, yellow-beaked, iridescent blackbirds who inhabit city streets, suburban yards, and farm fields with equal ease. In winter they become heavily speckled with white. Starlings are among the most widely distributed and successful birds on this continent—but they didn't originate here.

They evolved in Europe, increasing their numbers as human agriculture grew and becoming a pest species when human beings began to congregate in cities, which offered starlings central places to gather and roost in great numbers. They arrived in the United States in 1890 courtesy of an idealistic but ecologically naive drug manufacturer by the name of Eugene Scheifflin. Mr. Scheifflin's ambition was to bring all the birds mentioned in Shakespeare's works to the United States. He had not been discouraged by his earlier failures with chaffinches, song thrushes, skylarks, and nightingales, nor by the failures of earlier attempts to import starlings as insect controls.

The key to Scheifflin's "success" with starlings was not his superior motive, but an accident of time and place. He released his first thirty pairs in New York City—in Central Park—during what must have been a good year for starlings. Within a few weeks, the first nest was spotted under the eaves of the nearby American Museum of Natural History. In 1891, Scheifflin released forty more birds in Central Park, and it wasn't long before exploratory starlings began moving into Connecticut and New Jersey. They appeared in Vermont in 1913, reached California by 1942, and are now established even in central Alaska.

These days most people—especially farmers, orchardists, city planners, and airport personnel—consider starlings unmitigated pests. Even bird lovers become short-tempered with them during the nesting season because these aggressive imports drive native bluebirds and purple martins away from nesting cavities.

During the nesting season, however, starlings bother human communities less than at other times of the year because they operate in pairs rather than in flocks and they eat vast numbers of insects. From the time the first brood leaves the nest, though, the trouble begins again as small flocks of new young congregate and look for food resources they can share. By the end of the nesting season, the flocks are huge and can do considerable damage to farm fields.

Starlings have done well in the United States for a combination of reasons. First of all, they were introduced to an environment that had already been altered in much the same way that their European environment had been altered. Starlings thrive where natural ecosystems have been disrupted—as they are when cities are built. Also, starlings can nest in almost any cavity, they compete successfully for both nesting sites and food, and they produce two broods of young each year. Furthermore, they learn fast and change their behavior readily to meet new circumstances. As a final advantage, each individual starling benefits from the rest of the flock because the whole flock shares the tasks of food-finding and group protection.

If starlings hadn't begun to displace some of our native species and become a problem to human beings by virtue of their flocking and roosting habits, they might be looked at as avian versions of the American Dream. They have indeed established themselves on every part of this continent where the American Dream has led human beings.

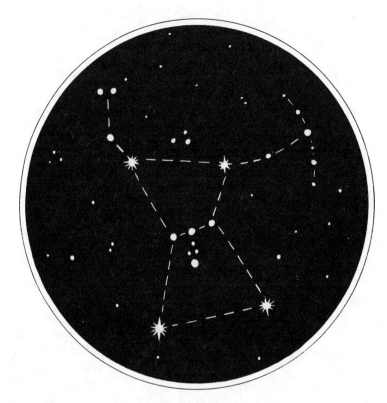

# ORION
## *Learning to Enjoy Winter Stargazing*

On clear winter nights, the stars seem especially bright. If you haven't done much stargazing, Orion is a good constellation to look for because he is easy to find. Before you learn to recognize him on sight, you can always find him by locating the Big Dipper and doing an about-face. There stands Orion, dominating the southern sky.

Orion is outlined by four bright stars at the corners of an imaginary trapezoid. Within the space defined by these four points, and seeming to draw them together into a pattern, is a row of three stars tilted at an angle—Orion's belt. Arcing downward from the belt is another group of fainter stars—his sword. Astronomers with good eyesight and a thorough knowledge of the night sky can point out a club above Orion's right shoulder and a lion's skin shield on his left arm.

Orion's story, like many of the stories from Greek mythology, is a melodrama. Several different legends surround him, but they all involve love, jealousy, revenge, and tragic death. Orion's first love affair was thwarted by the father of his bride-to-be. Even after Orion had slain the requisite beasts, the father refused to hold the wedding. So Orion raped his fiancée and was blinded by her father. This episode is only the beginning of his legend.

After regaining his sight, Orion took up with Artemis, goddess of the hunt. They spent a lot of time hunting together and forming a fond friendship. But Artemis's brother, Apollo, feared for his sister's affections. There are two different stories of how Apollo arranged for Orion's death. In one the jealous brother presses a giant scorpion into service. In the other he challenges Artemis to shoot an arrow at a distant target bobbing on the ocean, and the target turns out to be Orion's head. However Orion may have died, Artemis was so grief-stricken that she had him placed in the sky to be seen and remembered forever. And that's why, according to the Greeks and early astronomers, we have a giant hunter among our stars.

The major stars that constitute Orion offer examples of several different celestial phenomena. The bright star on the upper left, which is Orion's right shoulder, is called Betelgeuse—derived from an Arabic word meaning "shoulder of the giant." Through binoculars, it looks reddish-orange. The reddish color means this star is cooler than other stars, cooler even than our sun. Although Betelgeuse is cool, however, it still radiates a tremendous amount of light because it's huge. It is classified as a supergiant because it has a diameter greater than one hundred times the diameter of the sun—in this case, about four hundred times greater. Betelgeuse would completely fill the earth's orbit if it were at the center of our solar system.

Diagonally across the constellation, marking Orion's left foot, is a bright star called Rigel, from the Arabic word for "foot." It is smaller than Betelgeuse, but it is brighter because its surface temperature is hotter. One estimate places the temperature at close to 20,000° C, as opposed to 6,000° C for the surface of our sun and 3,000° C for the cooler surface of Betelgeuse. Rigel is classified as only a giant because its diameter is less than one hundred times that of the sun—only about thirty-three times.

Another noteworthy phenomenon in the constellation is the hazy area in the middle of Orion's sword. Through binoculars, this hazy area looks quite different from the stars above and below it. It is what's called a *diffuse nebula*—a mass of luminous gases and dust. Astronomers believe that gas clouds such as the Orion Nebula may represent stars in the process of being born.

Stargazing in winter might not be as leisurely as it is in summer, but something about it is more clarifying.

# CHICKADEES
## *Learning to Observe Backyard Birds—I*

$O$n a winter morning it's easy to linger over breakfast, half hypnotized by the chickadees at the bird feeder. Each one zooms in, perches nervously, grabs a seed, and dashes back out. Sometimes one chickadee doesn't move fast enough, and another flies in to displace it before the first one has gotten its seed. Sometimes two land at once, and one drives the other off, then grabs a seed. Sometimes two or three are lined up waiting for an opening. And all this happens at top, nonstop speed.

These winter flocks of chickadees are governed by strict laws of social order. The flitting in and out is a product of hierarchical laws interacting with the more democratic urgency of appetite. With all appetites equal and each bird having to give way to others in accordance with its status in the flock, food-getting requires both vigilance and haste. The exact power structure is hard to discern because all chickadees—young and old, male and female—look alike, but the petty squabbles when two or three birds arrive at the feeder simultaneously dramatize the individuals' relationships within the hierarchy.

It's hard to examine just one chickadee because they are all in constant motion. If you isolate one physical feature at a time, however, and watch for it on the next several individuals who land at your feeder, you can observe details. First of all, when you consider the shape of a chickadee's body, you will notice that it's round. Whereas a blue jay is elongated, and a nuthatch tapered and slightly flattened, a chickadee is like a little ball. This roundness helps the small bird balance itself in the topsy-turvy positions it assumes while it's searching for insect eggs on the twigs and outer branches of trees.

A chickadee couldn't perform its acrobatics without its feet. The strong little toes that grasp the edge of the feeder can also support the weight of the bird while it's hanging upside down from a twig. These feet give the chickadee its own place among the birds who search trees for hidden insects. While woodpeckers, nuthatches, and creepers climb up or down the tree's trunk, the chickadee dances among its twigs. A chickadee can also use its clever feet like hands. If you watch a chickadee eat a sunflower seed, you will see it hold the seed against its perch with its feet while it cracks the shell with its beak.

The short conical beak, which seems almost a part of the black cap that covers a chickadee's head and eyes, is also essential to the bird's eating habits. In addition to serving as a nutcracker and pick for the seeds it eats, the small, pointed beak is just the right size and shape for extricating insect eggs from their hiding places.

The beak has yet another use at nesting time. Both male and female chickadees peck rotting wood from a gray birch stub to create a nesting cavity. While woodpeckers leave their chips where they fall, chickadees transport what they've excavated to a distance so predators will not be alerted to the locations of their nests.

As you watch the chickadees' ceaseless activities outside

your kitchen window, your own life may seem leisurely by contrast. Human beings are subject to the same biological laws that govern chickadees, but fortunately our metabolisms and social structures allow us to operate at a somewhat slower pace.

# BLUE JAYS
## *Learning to Observe Backyard Birds—II*

*D*uring the winter, blue jays travel in small unstructured groups. These handsome, crested birds are bigger, bolder, and take more seeds than most of the other feeder birds. On each trip to the feeder, a blue jay collects as many seeds as it can fit into its gullet—usually fifteen or so—and then flies off to eat a few and hide, or perhaps bury, the rest. Whereas most other birds eat whatever food they can find immediately, the crafty blue jay eats what it wants and spreads the rest around so it's no longer concentrated in one place. One researcher theorizes that this behavior is not so much food storage as food dispersal, designed to discourage competitors from congregating at a good food source.

While a blue jay is at your feeder, either eating seeds or cramming them into its gullet, you can examine some of its adaptations. Its beak is long, sharp, and strong. This beak can crack the hard shell of an acorn as well as the softer shell of a sunflower seed. It can also catch insects, or, in rarer instances, rip the flesh of a small animal or baby bird. Blue jays have a bad reputation among bird lovers because they sometimes eat the eggs and young of other species, but food studies have shown that such predations account for less than one percent of the blue jay's largely seed-and-insect diet.

Basically, blue jays are omnivorous and opportunistic—they eat what's available when it's available—which gives them an advantage over birds who are more specialized in their diets. Their favorite wild foods are acorns and beechnuts (some of which they bury, inadvertently planting trees), and grasshoppers, beetles, and caterpillars, some of which might otherwise damage plants.

Attractive black and white markings draw your attention to a blue jay's wings and tail. The wings are short, reaching only the base of the tail when folded, and the tail is long. If you watch a blue jay fly, you will see how the short, rounded wings and long, fan-shaped tail help it cover short distances quickly and also enable it to twist skillfully among the branches of trees.

Another of the blue jay's well-known attributes is its voice. Many people think of blue jays as raucous and noisy, but if you listen you will hear a variety of sounds. Some of their calls are loud, insistent jeers that do become irritating if they go on and on, but others are more songlike tweedles, whistles, or whispers. Some of their phrases sound questioning or comical, like odd little remarks emanating from the woods. In addition to their own considerable repertoire, blue jays also imitate the sounds of other birds, including the cry of the red-shouldered hawk.

Finally, blue jays offer warning calls. They compensate for whatever damage they might do to other birds and animals with their occasional predations by issuing loud warnings when other predators enter the neighborhood. If you ever hear a group of blue jays making a racket near where you are, look for them and you may see a hawk or an owl. Blue jays like to harass predatory birds. They can afford to tease because they outnumber the bird they're picking on, and they are fast and skillful fliers.

Although blue jays are common birds, they are not the least bit ordinary. They are flexible, aggressive, resourceful, opportunistic, intelligent, and, according to bird classifiers, highly evolved. Blue jays are easy to see because they are not afraid of us, and they are worth observing for what they can teach us of avian success.

# BLACK BEARS
*Learning to Understand Animal
Behavior*

During the coldest part of winter, when human beings might be beginning to wonder whether they're going to survive—psychologically as well as physically—black bears are doing an amazing thing. The females are giving birth to their young and nursing these helpless, hungry creatures while their own bodies remain essentially asleep.

If bears were true hibernators, which is a popular misconception based on the sleepy winter bears of children's stories, this phenomenon wouldn't be possible. A true hibernator—such as a woodchuck—is in an almost deathlike torpor. Its body temperature is drastically reduced, and the heartbeat slows to only a few beats per minute. If brought indoors, a woodchuck awakens only very slowly, its body having to reactivate gradually before it becomes alert to its surroundings.

A winter black bear is more than just dozing, but it's not in the deep sleep of true hibernation. Its body temperature has dropped less than ten degrees, and its heartbeat has dropped from its waking rate of forty or fifty beats per minute to about ten. It awakens quite readily in response to a disturbance and can fall back asleep without much difficulty. This semi-hibernation is what enables the female black bear to give birth to her young and to provide them with the few attentions they need before curling her warm body around them and sinking back into her energy-conserving sleep.

The female black bear's body is in a strange physiological state after her young are born. Like the male, she gorged herself on nuts, acorns, and fruits during the late summer and fall to fatten herself for the long winter ahead. Before entering their separate winter dens, both males and females fasted for a period to clear their digestive systems. As a final preparation for their inactive winter, they ate pine needles, dry leaves, and a bit of their own hair to form a large plug to block the rectum.

Throughout the winter, black bears of both sexes live off their stored fat and reabsorb their wastes, saving themselves the trouble of eating, digesting, urinating and defecating. But while their digestive and excretory systems are inoperative, the female's reproductive system is still functional. Her mammary glands produce milk, and she nurses her newborn young—usually two of them—while the rest of her body continues to sleep for another eight to ten weeks.

This "sleeping motherhood" is the black bear's way of balancing the adults' problems with winter against the young's need to feed, grow, learn, and fatten in time for their own problems with the next winter. When black bear cubs are born in late January or early February, they are between a chipmunk and a squirrel in size. Their eyes and ears are closed, and only a fine fur covers their bodies. It takes almost a month for their eyes to become functional, a month and a half for their ears to open, and two months for them to learn to walk. Only at three months of age are they ready to leave the den and begin learning about the rest of the world.

As we wrestle with what's left of winter and yearn for spring, we might think about the female black bear sleeping in her den. She survives the season calmly by dividing her response. While her own sleeping body waits out the rest of winter, her young are her way of anticipating spring.

# GREAT HORNED OWLS
## Learning to Observe Owl Anatomy

*W*hile it's still winter, the largest of our native owls mate and lay their eggs. Great horned owls must start their family life in January or February in order to raise their single brood before the weather turns cold again at the other end of summer.

Great horned owls save themselves a little time at the outset by borrowing a nest rather than building one. They use the old nests of red-tailed hawks, herons, crows, or even squirrels. The prospective parents might tidy up the nest a bit, hollow out the center, and spread some of their own feathers inside, but otherwise they don't bother to build or rebuild the structure that will hold their eggs.

Incubation can last from twenty-six to thirty-five days, but even after all that time, the young owls hatch blind, helpless, and in need of complete care for several more weeks. It takes about ten weeks for them to grow their first flight feathers, and only then can the parents begin to teach them the difficult art of catching live prey.

The young owls learn a lot from their parents, but they also come equipped with certain basic adaptations. Their eyes, for instance, are especially adapted for focusing on moving prey. They are set like human eyes—looking directly forward—which gives them a wide range of binocular vision and good depth perception. These eyes are fixed in their sockets, but the owl's neck is extremely flexible, enabling it to turn and see things to the side and rear.

The owl's eyes are also adapted for night vision. They are lined with numerous light-sensitive cells, and even very dim light—such as the light of a candle burning over a thousand feet away—is enough for the owl to be able to catch a mouse. These same eyes function just as well in daylight, so the owl can hunt by day if it hasn't found enough food at night.

To complement these specialized eyes, the great horned owl also has specialized ears. The feather tufts, or "horns," on its head may look like ears, but they have nothing to do with hearing. The real ears are long slits hidden among the feathers on the sides of the owl's head. These slits, because they are asymmetrically placed, admit slightly different sounds to each of the owl's large eardrums. The size and arrangement of the ears help the owl pinpoint the origin of even very faint sounds—like the rustle of a mouse in the leaf litter.

Once the owl has seen or heard its prey, it is ready to fly in for the kill. Specialized wing feathers enable the large bird to move soundlessly through the air. The flight feathers are soft on the edges, so there's no sound of air rushing through them as the owl descends on its prey. Finally, the owl has strong, sharp talons, one of which can be rotated either forward or backward to help it catch and then carry the animal it's going to eat.

Throughout the summer and even into the fall, while the young are learning to be the fierce and successful predators they are destined to be, they still cry out to be fed. Some of the eeriest hoots heard during this period are not the threats of bloodthirsty killers but rather the hunger cries of young owls who would rather be fed by their parents than hunt for themselves. The parents eventually tire of these continuing demands, and with the approach of winter they complete their annual cycle. They drive their young out of the family territory, forcing them to start lives of their own.

# BEGINNING
## TO BE SPRING

## MAPLES
### *Learning to Observe Closely Related Trees*

*I*n areas that produce maple syrup, it's easy to identify maple trees from the end of February until April. They're the ones with the sap buckets attached. But at other times of the year, or in areas where people don't sugar, how do you recognize a maple? And how do you distinguish one species of maple from another?

One way to identify trees is by their silhouettes—the characteristic shapes created by the trunk and branches. Maples growing in a sugar bush or in the woods are frequently too close together for their shapes to show, but roadside maples and single maples growing in people's yards offer classic silhouettes. Of the two species that are important to sugarmakers, the sugar maple's silhouette is oval-shaped like an egg, while the red maple's is an elongated oval more like a watermelon.

After you've spotted an "egg" and a "watermelon," you're ready to move in closer to learn some of the other differences between these two closely related species. If you cut a short length of twig from each tree, you can examine them side by side, comparing and contrasting details. The sugar maple's twig is smooth, shiny, and tan, with tight, pointed buds, while the red maple's is bumpy, gray, and red toward the tip, with round, blunt, reddish buds. The two twigs hardly seem related, but the arrangement of the buds and scars from last year's leaves shows their kinship. Both buds and leaf scars are directly across from each other in pairs. This arrangement makes these *opposite* twigs—in contrast to the other possibility, which is called *alternate.* On alternate twigs, the buds are staggered, one growing on one side, the next growing higher up on the other. Only maples and a few other species of native trees produce their buds, leaves, twigs, and branches opposite each other, so it's a useful characteristic to note early in your examination of a tree.

The twigs of the sugar and red maples confirm the identifications you made from a distance, but it's still a good habit to observe whole trees in their surroundings. Although the two species of maples often grow close together, the sugar maple prefers drier soils than the red maple. The red maple, in fact, is commonly called the swamp maple because it grows in wet soils near swamps and rivers.

As spring proceeds, you can watch for other differences that will help you distinguish the two species. The red maple's flowers will be quite visible because they appear before the leaves open. From a distance they make the tree appear to be tinged with red, while close up you will see that they hang from the twigs like small red bangles. The sugar maple's small flowers will be yellowish, but they will be more difficult to see. They are hidden by the simultaneous appearance of leaves.

When the leaves of both species have appeared, you can contrast them, too, noticing the smooth outline of the sugar maple's leaf and the toothed outline of the red maple's. When the leaves change colors in the fall, you can watch the sugar maple turn to a mixture of brilliant yellows, oranges, and reds, while the red maple will turn to solid scarlet.

Looking closely at these two common species of maples, and comparing and contrasting their characteristics, will help you look intelligently at other trees. Most field guides offer a combination of pictures and words to help you identify different species, but the pictures and words won't make much sense until you've acquainted yourself with living trees.

# RACCOONS
## Learning to Observe Mammal Adaptations

*T*he muddy weeks that mark the end of winter and the beginning of spring are the ideal time for observing animal tracks. One of the most distinctive of these is the handlike print of the raccoon, which shows five slender toes and a flat, palmlike heel. Look for raccoon tracks near brooks, swamps, beaver ponds, and other wet places, or even in your own backyard or local park.

Raccoons don't spend their winter in the deep, inactive sleep of hibernation as woodchucks do. Like bears, they doze and sleep during most of the cold weather and have only the summer's accumulation of body fat to sustain themselves. Come spring, they're hungry, and they're also in a hurry to start their families. The female's gestation takes about sixty-three days, and her young depend on her for another four months. If she is to produce a reasonably fat generation before cold weather returns, she needs to get an early start.

The first raccoons out of their winter dens are the males. They wander in search of females, many of whom are still dozing in their dens, surrounded by their last year's young. Early spring is a confusing time of year for raccoons because last year's family groups are breaking up, males are looking for as many females as will have them, females aren't interested in additional males once they've mated, and everyone is hungry. As soon as the mating season is over, however, raccoon life settles into less stressful patterns. Males will forget about females and whatever young they have begotten and devote themselves entirely to eating. Females will also do their fair share of eating, spending long night hours foraging while their dependent young sleep and grow.

Raccoons are exceptionally well suited to the shifting, changing lifestyles required by the twentieth century. They are doing as well now as they were before European settlers arrived. Their most distinctive adaptation is their handlike feet. These feet enable them to walk, swim, and climb with equal ease, giving them more choices of food and shelter than most wild animals have. They can also use their front feet to turn over stones, reach into crevices, catch and hold small animals, manipulate inanimate objects—such as garbage can lids and door handles—and perform other manual tasks necessary to finding both wild foods and human garbage.

Just as their agile "hands" help them find numerous things to eat, their teeth enable them to eat just about anything they put into their mouths. Technically, raccoons are *carnivores*—that is, flesh eaters—but their teeth do not limit them to a diet of flesh. They have sharp canines like dogs and cats, which help them rip flesh, but they also have flattened molars, which enable them to chew and grind vegetable food. Raccoons enjoy a diet as mixed and omnivorous as the human diet, a fact they remind us of by raiding our garbage cans and soliciting handouts from our kitchens. They are equally happy, though, with such wild delicacies as crayfish, frogs, insects, and acorns. One way or another, raccoons have always found plenty to eat—and have always eaten it.

One zoologist suggests that the raccoon's agile hands give it the potential to evolve a technological descendant, should something happen to eliminate the human species. It's an interesting thought, but it's hard to imagine an animal who uses its hands so much for finding, manipulating, and fondling what it's about to eat evolving the right motives to operate a machine. It seems more likely, should something happen to us, that raccoons might use their agile hands to dismantle our technological civilization in search of one last hidden meal.

# PIGEONS
## *Learning to Observe Bird Adaptations*

*W*hile you're waiting for the redwings and robins to come back, you can entertain yourself by watching pigeons. They too will soon be courting and nesting as befits the season, and with so many other species in transit during the early weeks of spring, it is convenient to focus on these permanent residents.

All the pigeons currently inhabiting our farms, towns, and cities are descendants of wild rock doves, who were domesticated five to six thousand years ago by Near Eastern cultures. Pigeons were originally kept to be eaten. As cliff nesters, they adapted readily to the chinks and niches they found around human habitations. Eventually, they even accepted structures built especially for their nesting convenience. These early pigeon houses, called *dovecotes*, had one opening to the outside so the parents could come and go, and another to the inside so young pigeons, called *squabs*, could fall into a trough. These tender young birds were considered a great delicacy.

Somewhat later, human pigeon-keepers noticed that these gentle birds had a strong homing instinct, and pigeons became message carriers. Later still, pigeon fanciers began breeding them for unusual physical appearances. Some pigeons have been kept in domestication, but many have returned to an independent existence and become the melting-pot pigeons who congregate near human communities.

These multicolored, semi-tame birds share certain identifying characteristics with their wild relatives. Members of the pigeon family, which includes pigeons and doves, do two things that distinguish them from other birds. The first is that they drink water with their heads down. It doesn't sound like much, but other birds have to tilt their heads back to swallow. A pigeon merely dips its beak into water and sucks. The second pigeon accomplishment is the production of pigeon's milk. Surprisingly, this milk is produced by both males and females, and equally surprisingly, it is very much like mammalian milk, having almost the same composition as a female rabbit's. It is produced in the pigeon's crop—an enlarged storage area in its esophagus. The parent regurgitates it to feed the newly hatched young. The hormone that triggers the production of pigeon's milk, *prolactin*, is not unique to pigeons. In other birds it motivates brooding, while in mammals it signals lactation, or the release of milk to the young.

Because there is a limit to how much pigeon's milk a single pair of pigeons can produce, there is a limit to the size families they can raise. Most pigeons lay only two eggs at a time. The parents' milk lasts about ten days. By this time the young are already eating adult food, which the parents partially digest and regurgitate for them. The father then takes over feeding and teaching the first two young, while the mother prepares to lay another two eggs. Wild pigeons produce two or perhaps three broods in a season, but with the encouragement of human beings, who feed them throughout the year, some urban pigeons produce seven to eight broods in a year. This unnatural productiveness, coupled with the absence of natural predators in urban environments, accounts for the huge flocks of pigeons that thrive in many cities around the world.

When pigeons take flight, tails fanned and wings beating in short, powerful strokes, it is easy to envision their wild, cliff-dwelling ancestors. The original rock doves evolved great skill in flight because they had to outmaneuver their natural predators, the falcons, in order to survive as a species. Ironically, in today's world, we have more cause to worry about the survival of the falcons than the survival of the increasingly numerous pigeons.

# RED-WINGED BLACKBIRDS
## Learning to Understand Flock Behavior

*A*lthough the robin is the traditional symbol of spring, red-winged blackbirds actually return to the North earlier. When you catch a glimpse of red shoulder patches or hear the loud "o-ka-lee" of a redwing, you can be sure—no matter what the weather is doing—that it's spring.

The first flocks of redwings are headed farther north. These earliest flocks are males, traveling to places where they have nested in the past. Resident males begin to arrive a little later. By the second or third week in March, many of New England's resident males are back and establishing their territories.

Redwings congregate in and near marshy areas for their nesting. An entire flock of males will assert its claim to a chosen area, but within that area each male will establish his own territory and defend his boundaries against other males. The size of the individual territories depends on the space available and the number of males trying to share it. Redwings are capable of living quite close to one another as long as they honor their flockmates' boundaries.

While the resident males are working out their territorial claims, flocks of migrant females might stop in to visit them on their way farther north. The males, who are not yet ready to mate, drive them away. Anywhere from one to five weeks after the resident males have arrived, the resident females begin to show up. At first the males will try to drive them out, too, but these females are more persistent. Each keeps coming back to the place where she'd like to build her nest. The male whose territory includes the nesting site will eventually notice her, chase her around a bit, and finally claim her as a mate.

Some redwings are monogamous and some are polygamous. The male is not a collector of females, but because females frequently outnumber males, he is willing to take on a few extras if necessary. What seems more important to him than the number of his females is that other males stay out of his territory. In experiments to demonstrate how attached individual males and females are to each other, a nest was moved slowly out of a male's territory. Once the nest was outside his territorial boundary, he had no further interest in it or in the female who went with it. When, on the other hand, another nest belonging to a different female was moved slowly into his territory, he accepted and defended this newcomer as if she had been in his territory all along.

During the time redwings are nesting, they catch millions of insects to feed their young, which should make them welcome wherever they settle. But redwings are a mixed blessing. Later in the summer, just as the corn is ripening, large flocks of them will invade local fields, nibble at the corn, and become pests. And if Northerners think they have problems, they should visit the South during winter, when congregations of red-winged blackbirds join ranks with other birds for winter roosting. These huge roosting flocks do disproportionate damage to crops and peace of mind wherever they settle.

The problem posed by blackbird roosts is very complex. If only some of the birds are killed, there tends to be a higher survival rate among the young born the next summer, and by the next fall, populations are right back up to where they were. And if we destroyed all the birds in an attempt to solve fall and winter blackbird problems, we would soon have more serious problems with spring and summer insects. Whatever damage red-winged blackbirds do as they live out their seasonal cycles, we must find a way to balance our interests with theirs—or we'll discover that large blackbird populations were, after all, preferable to yet larger populations of insects.

# SPARROWS
## *Learning to Observe Sparrows*

Sparrows are bewildering. They are small, brown, streaked, and, to a beginning bird watcher, totally indistinguishable from each other. Then there's the imported English sparrow, which looks like our native sparrows and has given them a bad name. Technically, it's not even a sparrow—it's an Old World weaver finch. Just to confuse matters further, there's the female purple finch, who looks like a sparrow, only bigger, and female redwings, who are brown, streaked, and bigger still.

To keep yourself from becoming frustrated when you're beginning to learn about sparrows, limit your early efforts at identification to just those sparrows who visit your yard. You can scatter mixed seed on the ground to encourage them. While these hungry little birds are feeding, you'll have a good chance to look closely at their markings, and between visits you'll have plenty of time to consult your field guide. During your first year, try to master identification of at least two species, and each year after that add another one. Eventually, you will have to visit more distant spots to find a new sparrow, but maybe by then you'll feel ready.

Your first two species of sparrows might conveniently visit your yard at the same time, and as they feed side by side you will have no difficulty telling them apart. Their streaked backs will let you know they're sparrows, but you want to concentrate on their fronts. One of these common sparrows will have a plain gray breast with a single dark dot in the middle. The other will have a heavily streaked breast—brown on white—some of the streaks converging to form a dark spot toward the center. This rather major difference in the appearance of the two sparrows will alert you to a host of other small differences.

The gray-breasted sparrow has a rusty cap, a gray line above each eye, and a rust-colored line running through each eye. The streaked-breasted sparrow has a darker brown cap with a line of gray down the center, another line of gray above each eye, and a dark line through each eye. These alternating colors make the head look more striped than capped. When this second sparrow looks directly at you, you will see dark lines hanging down from either side of its beak, looking very much like a rooster's wattles.

Once you have looked closely at the two sparrows' markings, you should have no trouble at all using a field guide to identify the sparrow with the gray, unstreaked breast as a tree sparrow and the sparrow with the heavily streaked breast as a song sparrow. And once you have learned their names, you will be amazed to discover what different birds they are. The tree sparrow, for instance, is only a winter visitor to the northern half of the United States. In spring, it heads back to Canada to nest in the brushy areas where trees give way to tundra. Each pair will raise one brood during the brief northern summer and then head south again for winter.

The song sparrow, in contrast, nests throughout the Northeast, and each pair will raise two or three broods. Toward the end of October, most of them will head toward the southern United States for winter—shortly after the tree sparrows have begun arriving from the North. It's only during the transitional weeks of spring and fall that you're likely to find these two species feeding side by side and available for comparison.

Of the sparrows that might be seen in any one area, some are winter visitors, some are nesters, and some merely pass through in migration. A local checklist that indicates seasonal presence will help you determine which sparrows you should be looking for when. After you've mastered identification of the species that will visit your yard for mixed seeds, you can learn about preferred habitats and go out looking for the others.

# MOURNING CLOAKS
## *Learning to Look at a Butterfly*

*T*he signs of spring are everywhere by late March, and one of the most reassuring is the appearance of a butterfly. During a woodland walk at this time of year you might be surprised by the flutter of dark wings moving among the barren trees like one last falling leaf. The mourning cloak butterfly is named for its dark brown, velvety wings, but it is best known for its early spring appearances.

The mourning cloak's dark wings are edged with cream and decorated by a single row of blue dots just inside the edging. Its body is large and fuzzy brown, with two clubbed, white-tipped antennae projecting from its head. This handsome butterfly's annual cycle explains its early spring appearance.

Most butterflies—except for the monarch, which migrates

to Mexico—spend the winter as eggs, larvae, or pupae. Come spring, they need to undergo a few more changes before they'll be ready to appear in full adult splendor. But the mourning cloak hibernates as an adult. The first warm days of the new season invite it out of its hollow log or other winter hiding place to fly around the woods in search of tree sap. These mourning cloaks will later sip nectar, pollinating flowers in the process, but when they first emerge, sweet sap dripping from broken twigs or branches is all they have to go on.

Feeding on nectar is a relatively modern evolutionary development, which has only been around as long as flowering plants have. Butterflies are therefore more modern insects than dragonflies and cockroaches, whose ancestors go back almost three hundred million years. Being modern insects, butterflies undergo a complete, four-stage metamorphosis from egg to larva to pupa to adult. Whereas the adults provide a necessary and beneficial service as pollinators, the larvae, known as caterpillars, can sometimes be quite destructive. They hatch from their eggs with chewing mouthparts, as opposed to the sucking mouthparts they will have as adults, and they feed voraciously on leaves, as opposed to the nectar they will sip delicately as adults. But caterpillars shouldn't be judged negatively. They are doing all the growing the insect will ever do, and their fat bodies provide protein-rich food for other animals, especially young and growing birds.

Adult butterflies are considerate of their offspring even if they don't pay any attention to them. The females lay their eggs on a preferred food source. Favorite foods for mourning cloak caterpillars include elm, willow, poplar, and hackberry leaves, so the mourning cloak female deposits her eggs on a twig of one of these trees. Mourning cloak caterpillars tend to stay together while they're growing and have been known to cause considerable damage, especially to elm trees. During their larval stage they are sometimes referred to as spiny elm caterpillars.

After a period of sustained eating and growing, the butterfly caterpillar is ready to enter the stage of its life cycle called *pupation*, during which the tissues that were the caterpillar will reorganize themselves into an adult butterfly. When the adult emerges from the pupal covering, which is called a *chrysalis*, it is fully grown, with wing patterns characteristic of the species, sucking mouthparts, and the sexual equipment for mating. Mourning cloaks usually produce two broods during the warm months of the year. Surviving adults hibernate in the fall and emerge at the end of winter in time to get an early start the next spring.

Later in the spring and summer, the mourning cloak will be outshone by more brightly colored butterflies, but in March and April it holds its own among the moths, flies, bees, and other early insects. This special end-of-the-winter butterfly offers a subtle promise of the rich and varied colors soon to come.

# TRAILING ARBUTUS
## Learning to Observe the Flowers
of Early Spring

$D$uring the early weeks of spring, the woods show more and more signs of renewed life. Some of the woodland wild flowers bloom almost as soon as the snow has melted. If you know where a certain species has bloomed in the past, you can go back to that spot day after day, waiting patiently for the first flower to appear. But if you're new to the woods, you can be more exploratory, taking a different walk each day until you chance upon your first spring wild flower. One of the earliest, if you're lucky enough to find it, is trailing arbutus.

It was an old tradition in New England to pick the small, sweet-smelling flowers of this early bloomer and bring them indoors to celebrate spring. But then arbutus began to disappear. Over-picking was only part of the problem—even more threatening was the destruction of arbutus habitats as roads, houses, and towns began to preempt the wooded areas where arbutus grew. In recent years, arbutus has been placed on the endangered-species list in parts of its range.

Trailing arbutus grows around the edges and in sunny openings of oak and evergreen woods. It grows equally well in sandy coastal soils and in shallow, rocky, upland soils, its primary requirement being acidity. It chooses oak or evergreen companions because they keep soils acid by littering the forest floor with their acidic leaves and needles. Given the right soil and the proper balance between sunlight and shade, trailing arbutus produces a woody, trailing, perennial stem that can grow a foot or more in length. Its leathery evergreen leaves are slightly bigger than a human thumbprint, and they feel like a fine grade of sandpaper to the touch.

Trailing arbutus is best known for its aromatic flowers, which offer sweet nectar to early spring insects and tempt human beings to pick them. The flowers, which are pink or white and look as if they're molded from wax, grow in clusters of four or five at the end of the trailing stem. They are tubular, but the tips of the five petals flare outward so that from above each flower looks like a small waxen star.

The flowers are only one stage of this perennial plant's life cycle. The evergreen leaves surrounding this year's flowers are last year's leaves. This year's will appear in June, long after the flowers have gone to seed. The seeds will, in fact, be ready to disperse about the time the new leaves grow.

While early spring insects pollinated the flowers as they sipped nectar, chipmunks, ants, slugs, and other woodland creatures will eat—and disperse—the seeds. Sometimes these animals carry a seed off and then forget to eat it. If the seed is left in suitably acidic soil, it might germinate. The seeds sometimes also find space for themselves near the parent plant, so that trailing arbutus left undisturbed tends to grow in expanding beds.

An arbutus seed takes a long time to germinate—maybe a month to six weeks—and after germination the plant takes another three years to flower and produce more seeds. This leisurely life cycle makes it hard to tell just how a struggling bed of arbutus might be doing, but once the new plants are established, they will grow year after year, gradually spreading themselves and producing more of their fragrant flowers to cheer us early each spring.

# GARTER SNAKES
## Learning to Understand Snakes

*I*f you take some of your early spring walks in rocky terrain, you might encounter an aggregation of garter snakes just emerging from hibernation. They will be lying on a sunny rock, draped all over each other like spaghetti. If you are afraid of snakes, overcome your fear long enough to look at this comfortable group. Looking at such nonthreatening creatures might help you rid yourself of your phobia.

Groups of early-spring garter snakes are a random assortment of individuals who congregated in the fall while they were searching for a good place to hibernate. The spring sun warms the rocks they are hiding under, and the heat reactivates their cold-blooded bodies enough for them to crawl out into the sun. During the time these emerging groups are still together, some in-

dividuals will mate. Then, having only chanced to winter together, they will all disperse in search of food. They will remain
solitary until cool weather signals them to hibernate again. The
only group of garter snakes you might see later in the summer
would consist of a female with her recently born young.

Garter snakes are the successful animals they are because
they aren't locked into narrow habitat choices or limited sources
of food. They live in the woods, in fields, on lawns, around stone
walls, in gardens, cemeteries, and parks. They eat frogs, toads,
salamanders, earthworms, insects, and sometimes even small
mammals or birds.

Because a garter snake has no limbs, it has to catch what it
eats in its mouth, and because it has no chewing teeth, it has to
swallow its prey whole. If you ever have the opportunity, watch a
garter snake eat a frog; it won't help you much with your snake
phobia, but it will show you how a snake's jaws work. The lower
jaw is specially hinged to enable it to stretch around prey larger
in circumference than the snake's body. Each half of the lower
jaw can move independently, and the two halves can stretch
apart, too. The snake's backward-slanting teeth serve no chewing
function. They merely keep the prey headed in the right direction as the versatile jaws work it in.

The garter snake's sensory equipment is designed to help
it detect either prey or danger and to react appropriately. The
fixed, unblinking eyes give the snake accurate vision for moving
objects. They are protected by a transparent layer of skin that fits
right over them like contact lenses.

If the snake's prey can hold still, it can avoid visual detec-
tion, but it can't help giving off odors. As the garter snake's forked
tongue flicks out, it picks up trace chemicals from the atmosphere.
When the tongue is flicked back in, the tips enter a special organ
in the roof of the mouth. This organ, called the *Jacobson's organ*,
analyzes the chemical substances and transmits "taste-smells" to
the snake's brain.

The garter snake's hearing is also unusual. The snake
doesn't hear the ordinary sounds in its environment or even loud
shouts, because it lacks external ear openings. But its internal ears
can perceive sounds of low frequencies, and its whole head and
body are sensitive to vibrations transmitted through the ground.

While many human beings are afraid of snakes for irrational reasons, a garter snake has good cause to be afraid of human beings. Our footsteps on a rocky trail are an uneven rumbling of what, to a snake's ears, must be huge and ominous vibrations. Then we are large, hovering presences that emit unfamiliar chemical signals. As you stand your ground and make yourself look directly at a garter snake—or an aggregation of them—in an attempt to overcome your phobia, you might occupy yourself by wondering whether those rapidly flicking tongues are sensitive enough to detect fear mixed with resolution.

# TADPOLES
## Learning to Observe Amphibian Metamorphosis

*A*s spring proceeds, ponds fill up with newly hatched tadpoles. For most of the spring and summer, these tadpoles look like dark little heads with whiplash tails, resembling punctuation marks more than baby frogs or toads. But a dramatic metamorphosis will change them from well-adapted aquatic young to equally well-adapted terrestrial adults.

When a tadpole first hatches from its egg, it's a helpless little blob with sightless eyes and no mouth. For several days it clings to the jelly mass of its egg cluster or to vegetation nearby. Small adhesive organs on the underside of its head enable it to hang on. As the new tadpole absorbs what's left of its egg yolk, the adhesive organs are lost, and the animal begins to look more like the tadpoles we're used to seeing. At this early stage, however, a tadpole has feathery external gills that it waves in the water to obtain oxygen.

The first changes the tadpole undergoes are not part of the metamorphosis into adulthood, but they are necessary to the young tadpole's success as an aquatic animal. Its mouth opens, and it develops a horny beak and rasping teeth to help it break and scrape vegetation for food. Its eyes are still small and flat against its head, but the corneas become clear so the tadpole can see underwater. Gill slits develop, and a fold of skin grows over the external gills. Eventually, the skin encloses the gills completely, creating internal gill chambers with a small hole on the left side where water that has come in through the tadpole's mouth can exit. Meanwhile, the tail lengthens to serve as the tadpole's means of locomotion. All these early changes take a week to ten days, depending on the species of the tadpole and the temperature of the water.

The first change that indicates the tadpole's future as a terrestrial adult is the appearance of two small hind legs. For the next five to six weeks the tadpole eats and grows without changing much more, but then the dramatic changes of metamorphosis begin. The tadpole's thyroid sends a hormone called *thyroxine* through the bloodstream to tissues throughout its body, and the different tissues begin to respond in different ways. The back legs grow longer quite rapidly, while the front legs develop more gradually inside the gill chambers. The left leg finally appears through the exit hole, and the right one breaks through the skin on the other side, which has been weakened by secretions from the degenerating gills. The gills, at this stage, are being superseded by lungs.

When both front legs are visible, the tadpole is ready to spend its last aquatic week undergoing the final changes that will prepare it to live on land. During this climax, so many changes happen at once that the tadpole can't eat and has to hover near the surface of the water for oxygen. The mouth widens, stretches backward, and loses its horny beak and rasping teeth in favor of a long tongue and real teeth. The eyes grow bigger, protrude from the head, change internally for out-of-water vision, and develop protective eyelids. Mucous glands form in the skin, the skeleton hardens into bone, and the long, coiled intestine that digested algae and other aquatic foods shrinks and changes into the short intestine of an insect-eater. To keep from starving while all these changes are completing themselves, the tadpole absorbs its own tail.

At the end of this massive changing of tissues and functions, the young frog or toad hops onto dry land to start the next stage of its life.

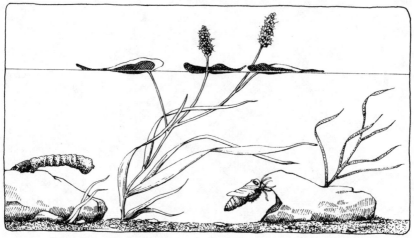

# BLACK FLIES
## Learning to Observe an Organism's Life Cycle

*I*nstead of looking at all insects as pests, it is wiser to identify the species or individuals who are most likely to bother you and then to avoid them. But some insects won't return the favor. Just when spring weather makes it most tempting to be outdoors, a certain species emerges from the rushing waters of cold streams to ruin nature walks, garden projects, and other outdoor enterprises.

The black fly is a fact of outdoor life. Mammalian blood—and the mammal, unfortunately, is often human—plays a key role in this insect's life cycle. That's where we wind up at cross-purposes. The problem is that female black flies, like their cousins, female mosquitoes, need a meal of blood to help them produce their eggs. The flower nectar, on which the males subsist, just doesn't provide enough protein.

Mosquitoes and black flies have similar piercing, sucking mouthparts, but a mosquito's bite seems gentle—almost courteous—in comparison to the black fly's. A female mosquito at least warns of her presence with her high-pitched whine, and she gives you a fair chance of swatting her or brushing her away because you feel a slight pinprick when she first pierces your skin.

The black fly, in contrast, is silent and secretive in her bite. A number of them hover around your head while a few strike. They usually attack outside your range of vision—behind your ears, for instance, on your scalp, or inside your collar. It's always difficult to appraise the total damage until hours later, when the bites swell, itch, and—if you scratch them too hard—begin to hurt.

Black-fly bites are much more bothersome than mosquito bites. They're bigger, they itch more persistently, and they last longer. Both mosquitoes and black flies inject an anticoagulant when they bite us to keep our blood from clotting while they're sucking it. The anticoagulant explains the swelling and the itching of the bites, but the black fly must inject more of it or use a stronger brand.

The bothersome, bloodsucking stage of the black fly's life cycle accounts for only one brief period of its existence. In the other stages it is no bother at all. The blood-fed female will eventually lay her eggs on rocks, sticks, or vegetation in or near a stream. These eggs will hatch into aquatic larvae, well adapted for life in fast-moving water. Each larva attaches itself to an underwater rock by means of hooks and a suction disk. The moving water then delivers food, saving the larva the trouble of traveling for or chasing its meals. From each larva's head protrude two stalks with rakelike bristles for filtering small food particles from the passing water.

After the larva has eaten, grown, and molted six or seven times, it spins a conical, open-ended cocoon, which it attaches securely to a rock—still underwater. Inside the cocoon, the insect pupates, changing from the aquatic larva to an aerial adult. Because wet wings would spell disaster to the emerging adult, the pupa produces an air bubble as the time approaches for the adult to climb out of the pupal skin. The winged insect then floats safely to the surface inside its air bubble, the bubble bursts, and the adult flies free.

North American black flies don't do any serious or permanent damage to human beings. They merely irritate us for a few weeks in the spring. Actually, they perform a useful service in helping us balance our attitudes toward the seasons. Just when we might be thinking that spring is much preferable to winter, black flies emerge in blood-hungry numbers to remind us of winter's cold and bug-free glory.

# SPRING

# COMMON BLUE VIOLETS
## Learning to Observe Pollination

*V*iolets are among the commonest spring wild flowers. The familiar purple species, called the common blue violet, grows in moist woods, along brooks, around the edges of damp meadows, and near houses. Children often pick whole bouquets of them, their short, thin stems being just the right size to clasp in a sweaty little hand. If violets were endangered, children would have to be taught not to pick them, but these tempting little plants can withstand a child's enthusiasm. Their strategy for survival includes a backup system that makes a certain number of the flowers expendable.

Early each spring, the perennial underground part of the plant, called the rhizome, sends up heart-shaped leaves and purple flowers, each leaf and flower on a separate stalk. These early flowers are the familiar five-petaled violets we notice and pick. They are quite showy because it's their job to attract insects for cross-pollination. The upper pair of petals stand like flags above the lower three. The lowest petal, which is also the longest, is the insect's landing platform. Streaks invite the insect to crawl toward the base of this petal, which extends behind the flower as a hollow, tubular spur. Some of the flower's male parts secrete nectar deep inside this spur.

When the insect reaches for the nectar, it disturbs other male parts, which then release some of their pollen. When the insect moves on to another violet and reaches into it for a taste of nectar, it deposits some pollen on the tip of this flower's female part. If all goes well, numerous violets are cross-pollinated by insects during this early flowering period, and a new generation of plants with genes from two separate parents will grow from the seeds.

But violets also have a backup plan to keep their own genes available even if they won't become mixed with another violet's during that particular growing season. After the showy flowers have disappeared, the plant produces another set that are difficult to see because they are small, compact, and grow close to the ground. These later flowers stay closed because they don't need insects to pollinate them. They are designed to pollinate themselves. These smaller flowers are often more successful than their insect-dependent predecessors, producing many more seeds.

Seed dispersal is another important component of any plant's strategy for survival. Both sets of violet seeds mature within a three-sectioned fruit, the fruit splits into its three sections, and each section begins to dry out. As it dries, it curls, putting more and more pressure on the numerous seeds inside until the skin splits and the seeds pop out, flying several feet away from the parent plant. Some of the violet's seeds will be eaten by mourning doves, ruffed grouse, bobwhite quail, wild turkeys, juncos, and white-footed mice, but many will germinate and produce new violets.

The more you study flowers, the more you will learn to admire the most common ones. The wild flowers that we learned the names of as children, or that we just seem to know about without consulting field guides, are for the most part flowers with highly successful reproductive schemes. Common blue violets may not be prized by anyone but children, but their strategy for survival is admirable from any point of view.

# NORTHERN ORIOLES
*Learning to Understand
Species Classification*

The year 1973 was a turning-point for Baltimore orioles. They got a new name that year. They were regrouped with their western counterparts, with whom they had been interbreeding, and given the more inclusive name of northern oriole. Although many people are still more comfortable with the old name, the new name is intended to reflect biological fact. The northern oriole's story, which goes back over ten thousand years, is representative of what has happened to many other species of plants and animals in North America. The story begins when the last of the glaciers drifted south from Canada into the northern United States.

The ice and cold climate pushed plants and animals southward, and some species found themselves divided by geographical barriers into southwestern and southeastern populations. Mountains, deserts, and the absence of northern forests kept them from meeting, mixing, and nesting together. When the glacier retreated, plants and animals gradually pushed northward again. But for woodland birds such as the oriole, the treeless Great Plains continued to act as a barrier, still separating populations that had begun to differentiate during the long years the glacier kept them apart.

Then settlers moved to the Great Plains and planted trees around their houses as windbreaks. These trees, combined with the trees that grew along river banks, offered orioles an appealing nesting habitat. Eastern orioles expanded westward and western orioles expanded eastward until they encountered each other in Kansas and Nebraska. Ornithologists observed that in the zone where the two different-looking orioles overlapped, they interbred quite readily. It seems that the length of time the two populations had been separated was sufficient to produce differences in appearance but not in courtship and nesting behavior. So the western oriole, which had been called the Bullock's oriole, and the eastern oriole, which had been called the Baltimore oriole, were reclassified as subspecies of a single species called, impartially, the northern oriole.

So nothing about the Baltimore oriole has changed except our understanding of it and therefore its name. The male is still the familiar orange and black bird that returns to the trees around suburban and country yards each spring to sing, whistle, buzz, chatter, and flash his brilliant colors, while the less visible female constructs the hanging pouch that will house their young.

The female's nest is almost as well known as the male's colors. To build it, she first finds some long fibers, which she loops and winds around the twigs that will support the nest. Then she brings more materials and begins attaching them randomly to these dangling lines. She doesn't actually weave one strand back and forth through the others. She merely pokes her latest addition through the web she's created so far, then reaches through with her beak to seize a loose end from the other side.

She works from what will be the inside of her nest, producing a strong, matted pouch in four to eight days. Toward the end of her weaving activities, she bounces around inside her nest, shaping it to fit her body. The finished product looks like a gourd and feels like burlap. Some old nests are so well constructed that they stay intact for years, becoming visible again each fall when the leaves drop off.

This familiar oriole has been returning to the North each spring and building its attractive nest since long before it had a name—let alone a name change. "Northern oriole" is merely a more inclusive title for a species that has always ranged quite a distance from Baltimore.

# GRACKLES
## *Learning to Understand*
## *Reproductive Strategies*

$S$ome people don't like grackles. Human sensibilities are offended by their rusty-hinge voices, their dark, oily colors, and their tendency to gather in noisy, hungry flocks. Even their name is harsh to human ears. But these long-tailed, yellow-eyed grackles—unlike the shorter-tailed, yellow-beaked starlings we imported from Europe—were here before we were. So it's up to us to come to terms with them.

Actually, most of the problems we have with grackles were brought on by our own practices. Before European settlers arrived on this continent, grackles nested near river floodplains and other natural openings in the forest. They fed on insects during the nesting season and on wild seeds, fruits, and nuts during the rest of the year. Their large roosts bothered no one because no one was around to be bothered.

With the coming of settlers, however, conditions changed. Land was cleared and planted with corn and other crops, creating circumstances much to the grackles' liking. They extended their range, following the pattern of agricultural expansion and, along with other flocking, seed-eating birds, such as red-winged blackbirds, they became agricultural pests.

Separate altogether from the grackles' interactions with human beings are their interactions with each other. They are basically colonial rather than territorial as individuals. They nest close together, both sexes defending only a small space immediately around the nest. The male doesn't help build the nest, which takes the female about five days, and he doesn't help incubate the eggs, which takes the female another thirteen to fourteen days, but he's there for the most strenuous task—twelve or more days of gathering insects to feed the growing nestlings.

Grackles employ a fairly complex scheme to assure that at least some of their young survive to the fledgling stage. If a female lays a small clutch of eggs—two, three, or four—the parents invest all their energy in raising all the young. Sometimes, however, a female lays five or six eggs, and then the adults have some options.

According to researchers who have weighed eggs and examined nestlings to determine their sex, the female produces bigger eggs that will hatch into males toward the end of her laying. With the smaller clutches, she begins incubating when she lays the final egg so that all the eggs hatch at once. With the larger clutches, in contrast, she begins incubating before the last eggs are laid so that the first eggs hatch before the bigger eggs. The nestlings that hatch early have the advantage of age, but the nestlings that hatch later have the advantage of more nourishment in the egg.

When all five or six nestlings have hatched, the parents can accommodate to the local food supply by either feeding all the nestlings, or, if food is short, letting the late-hatching males starve. The researchers call this strategy "hedging their bets." If it's a good year for insects, the pair might raise a large brood of healthy young with a few extra males, but if it's a bad year, they can raise at least as many young as the more conservative clutch would have produced.

Grackles have a public relations problem, not because of their behavior during the nesting season but because of their noisy and hungry descent upon farmers' fields when the nesting season is over. And their proud, unthreatened manner doesn't help them much either. Grackles don't respond to human presence by hiding in the woods and uttering high-pitched alarm notes. They stride boldly through the fields, pronouncing loud, assertive *"chacks."* With their black plumage and their bright yellow eyes, they just don't look as humble as most other birds do. But maybe we can learn something about our place in the natural order from birds who aren't humble.

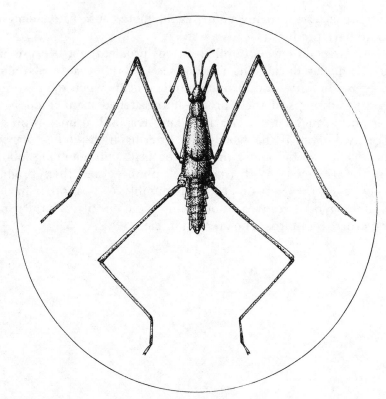

# WATER STRIDERS
### Learning to Observe
### an Aquatic Insect—I

*D*espite all the energy and motion of spring runoff, there always remain eddies where a swollen brook merely swirls and drifts. These backwaters are good spots to look for water striders. But you'll have to look carefully because on sunny spring days a water strider appears more shadow than insect. Its position on the water's surface camouflages its body, but the sun creates a pattern of six dark ovals that look like a strangely constructed pawprint on the brook's sandy bottom. The shadow moves with the water as if it were gliding along the bottom with the current, but then two of the small ovals sweep backward like oars, and the shadow propels itself into quieter water.

When you spot the shadow, all you have to do is focus on the water's surface and you'll see the insect. Its long legs make dimples where they touch the water and small ripples when they paddle to a new position. If you bend down and look from an angle, you will see an edge of white from the water strider's underside. A fish looking up from below has as much trouble seeing the white underside as you have seeing the dark back.

Close up, the water strider looks as if it has only four legs, but the shadow clearly indicates six. The front legs are just so small that they hardly show. They are held forward close to the antennae and are adapted for grasping prey. The second pair are long and quite visible because they're the oars. They either rest lightly on the water's surface or make sudden broad sweeps when the insect wants to move. The long rear legs hang back as if they're doing nothing, but they're actually the insect's rudder.

The water strider's whole existence depends on the physical phenomenon called *surface tension*. Molecules at the surface of water are linked together more tightly than molecules beneath the surface. If an object can avoid breaking the surface tension, it can glide across the thin film of closely connected molecules, but if any part of it breaks through, it will sink. A standard illustration of this phenomenon involves lowering a needle very gently onto the surface of a glass of water. If you are careful enough, the needle will float, but if any part of the needle breaks the surface tension, it will plummet to the bottom of the glass.

The water strider is better adapted for life on the surface of water than a needle is. Its long legs spread its weight over a bigger area, and brushy, waterproof hairs on its feet diffuse the points of contact. Its underside is also covered with waterproof hairs to keep the insect dry. The ease with which the water strider darts across the brook's surface shows how unlikely it is that this well-adapted insect will break through the film of molecules that supports it.

A water strider is a scavenger. It eats insects—dead or alive—that it finds floating on the water's surface. Most of its aquatic relatives prefer live food, so the water strider's role is important. It is part of the aquatic cleanup crew.

Adult water striders mate during the spring and early summer and lay their eggs on aquatic vegetation. The female covers them with a waterproof substance to protect them during the two weeks it takes before they hatch. The young sink to the bottom when they hatch, but they soon swim to the surface, looking very much like miniature adults. They eat, grow, and molt five times during the next month or so, and then they themselves are ready to mate. This gradual change from youth to adulthood is called an *incomplete metamorphosis*. It is a more primitive pattern of insect development than the complete, four-stage metamorphosis of flies, butterflies, and beetles.

Water striders generally produce two generations during the summer. The second generation hibernates under a log, stone, or vegetation near the brook during the winter, ready to emerge as soon as it's warm enough to resume their quiet lives on the brook's backwaters.

# WHIRLIGIG BEETLES
*Learning to Observe*
*an Aquatic Insect—II*

*F*rom a distance, whirligig beetles look like bubbles whirling around on the surface of a pond. Up close, however, you can see these shiny, round-backed insects speeding through tight S-curves and figure eights.

Their movements resemble those of the dodgem cars at an amusement park, only the beetles aren't trying to ram each other. Whirligig beetles are as well adapted as water striders to their life on the surface of water, yet these two insects are completely different in appearance, equipment, and life cycle. Part of the difference is explained by a difference in evolutionary history, and part by a slight difference in the relationship of the two insects to water.

While water striders belong to the relatively primitive order of insects called *true bugs*, whirligig beetles, as their name indicates, belong to the more modern order called *beetles*. True bugs are known as *hemipterans*, or "half wings," because their front wings are thickened where they join the body but membranous toward the tips. Beetles are known as *coleopterans*, or "sheath wings," because their front wings are hard and shiny, closing into a protective sheath over the insect's back. The whirligig beetle's rounded, shiny "back" is actually these protective wings.

For mouthparts, true bugs have piercing, sucking beaks that enable them to extract the juices of their prey—or, in some species, the juices of plants. Beetles, in contrast, have chewing mouthparts. Both water striders and whirligig beetles feed on other insects they find on or near the surface of water but, having different kinds of mouthparts, they eat their meals in different ways. The water strider pierces the insect's tough exoskeleton and sucks the juices, while the whirligig beetle chews on the whole insect, rejecting some parts and passing the rest into a special stomach where the meal is ground into a digestible mash.

True bugs experience an incomplete metamorphosis—young water striders merely grow and molt until they become adults, without ever changing dramatically in appearance. Whirligig beetles go through the four distinct stages of a complete metamorphosis. A whirligig beetle starts life as an egg laid on submerged vegetation and hatches into a larva that looks more like a centipede than an adult beetle. It has gills and lives underwater while it's growing. Toward the end of this stage it crawls out of the water, spins a small cocoon, and enters the third, or pupal, stage, where it rests for about a month. It emerges from its cocoon a fully formed whirligig beetle ready to take up adult life on the surface of a pond.

In addition to all these differences in appearance, equipment, and life cycle, the whirligig beetle also has a slightly different relationship to water. Whereas the water strider stands on long legs above the water, depending on its hair-tipped feet to keep it from breaking through the surface film, the whirligig beetle lives half on the surface and half just beneath it. The underside of its body is actually underwater, and its short legs propel it through the water rather than across the surface film. It even has special eyes to help it live this double life. Each eye is divided, one part above water to watch what's happening on the surface and one part below water to follow underwater activities. The whirligig beetle can also dive if it feels like it or fly to another part of the pond.

When different life forms adapt to similar living conditions, they sometimes begin to look and act like each other—a phenomenon called *convergent evolution*—but the water strider and whirligig beetle have not converged. They have instead evolved completely different ways of living successfully on the surface of water.

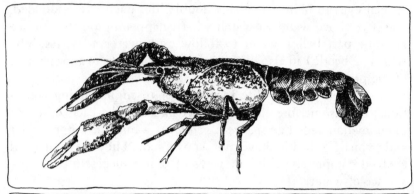

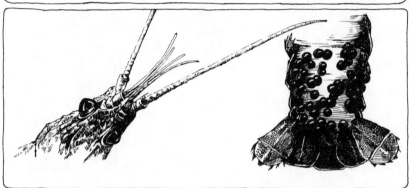

# CRAYFISH
## *Learning to Observe a Crustacean*

*I*f a warm spring day tempts you to take off your shoes and go wading in a brook, you might startle a crayfish, who will dash for a hiding place under a rock. This small aquatic creature, who looks like a miniature lobster, is a *crustacean.* Crustaceans are distantly related to insects—both have hard external coverings, called exoskeletons, and jointed legs—but crustaceans have an extra pair of antennae.

Crustaceans have much more than two sets of antennae to help them through life, but the extra pair, called *antennules,* are what distinguishes them from other animals. If you look down on a crayfish from above, which is how you'll probably see it if you're lucky enough to catch a glimpse of one of these shy creatures, you will see lots of other appendages. Altogether they have thirty-eight, but only the two pairs of antennae, one pair of pincers, and four pairs of walking legs show clearly from above.

The long, whiplike pair of antennae help the crayfish keep track of what's going on in front of and behind it. The shorter, branched pair are more attuned to things close by. Both are sensitive to touch and smell. The pincers, which are miniature versions of a lobster's claws, enable the crayfish to pick up food and to defend itself. The four smaller pairs of legs are for locomotion and digging.

A crayfish digs to hide itself from its many predators. In fact, it spends most of the daylight hours dug into a pebbly bottom or hidden under a rock. Because the crayfish is a medium-sized creature, it is an important link in many aquatic food chains. The crayfish scavenges its aquatic habitat for small plants and animals and, in turn, becomes food for fish, frogs, turtles, snakes, otters, minks, raccoons, and wading birds.

The only defense the crayfish has against these hungry animals, besides its protective coloration and its undersized pincers, is its ability to swim backward in a hurry. It flips its flexible abdomen forward in a way that propels it backward with a jerk. The suddenness of the motion sometimes surprises the predator and gives the crayfish time to find refuge under a rock.

To compensate for losses to predation, the female crayfish lays several hundred eggs. Crayfish mate in the fall, but the female doesn't lay the eggs until spring. When she does lay them, she glues them to abdominal appendages called *swimmerets* and carries them with her for the five to eight weeks until they hatch. When the young crayfish hatch, they hang onto their mother's swimmerets for several weeks until they have grown a bit and are ready to take up an independent existence.

To grow, a crayfish, like an insect, must shed its tough outer covering. The molt begins with the old exoskeleton splitting lengthwise down the back. The crayfish extricates itself from the protective but confining shell, then blows itself up to an expanded size so that the new covering will harden with space inside to grow. While the new covering is hardening, the crayfish is extremely vulnerable.

Crayfish are humble creatures, but they represent an adventurous line of evolution. While many of the larger crustaceans, such as lobsters, crabs, and shrimp, remained in the saltwater environments where they originated, crayfish made their way up estuaries and established a role for themselves among the plants and animals who inhabit fresh water.

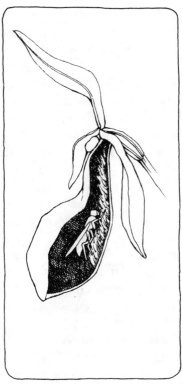

# PINK LADY'S SLIPPERS
## Learning to Observe an Orchid

$S$pring rains turn the countryside so green and lush that even northern areas can feel quite tropical. When you encounter an exotic pouched flower—an orchid—growing in the woods at this time of year, it's easy to imagine you've been transported several latitudes south. But temperate North America has its own native orchids, just as the tropics do. Some people call the species northern New Englanders see most often a pink moccasin flower, but "moccasin" doesn't seem right for the delicate construction of the pouched lower petal. Its other common name, the pink lady's slipper, is more descriptive.

Pink lady's slippers belong to the orchid family, which is a large and advanced family of flowering plants. Each species of orchid is different in appearance, but they all have certain growth habits, structures, and strategies in common. The pink lady's slipper offers just one example of how carefully orchids live.

Orchids are highly sensitive to their environments. Each species needs its own species of fungus growing on its roots in order to survive. An orchid seed, which is about the size of a dust particle and which may have traveled a great distance with the wind, will not even germinate unless the fungus it needs is present in the soil. Furthermore, each orchid has other environmental requirements. The pink lady's slipper, for instance, needs acidic soil that is well drained and shaded at least part of the time.

Despite an orchid's choosiness, the number of seeds produced by each plant assures a few success stories. And to encourage seed production, orchids have evolved amazingly complex flowers. Most flowers have petals that look like petals, but orchids have a special structure called a *lip*. In the pink lady's slipper, the lip takes the form of a large, air-filled pouch. This pouch is actually just one highly modified petal, but it goes beyond other petals in its appeal to insect pollinators. It invites the specific insect it's adapted to to land—and also to crawl inside. The orchid's intention is not to trap this insect but merely to detain it for a while and then to force it to exit by a different route.

The insect visitor—a small bee in the case of the pink lady's slipper—enters the pouch through the slit that runs full length down the front. Once through the slit, the bee can't crawl back out because of the close-fitting, inward-curving edges. But the bee doesn't want to leave immediately anyway. There are some appealing hairs inside the pouch, which the bee licks and eats before it's ready to think about extricating itself from this delicious place.

When it's ready to leave, the bee is attracted to light at the top of the pouch. The bee can't crawl straight out the top, however, because the combined male and female flower parts, called the *column*, stand in the way. The insect must crawl upward into the pouch's narrow neck, brush under the orchid's female part, turn left or right, and push its way out under one of the pollen-filled male parts. An orchid's pollen is packed into a sticky little ball, called a *pollinium*, which sticks to the insect when it leaves.

The orchid's whole purpose in manipulating the insect so carefully is to assure cross-pollination. When the pollen-laden bee enters the next lady's slipper, the pollen it's carrying on its back is ready to be scraped off as it first crawls under the female flower part on its way out again. Only then will it gather another pollinium as it squeezes under one of this flower's male parts. Many flowers depend on insects to pollinate them, but the orchid, with its exactly arranged flower parts, leaves little to chance.

## STINGING NETTLES
### Learning to Observe a Plant That Stings

*I*f spring has you wearing shorts and sleeveless shirts, you might get stung—not by insects but by a certain tall, nondescript plant that grows beside moist woodland trails and around gardens. You'll feel a sudden sting and then a prickly sensation that some people call the "seven-minute itch." The plant that causes this reaction is known as the stinging nettle. It belongs to a genus called *Urtica,* which derives its name from the Latin word *uro,* meaning "to burn." The stinging nettle is best known for the little stinging, burning welts it raises on human skin—which usually disappear well within seven minutes.

Stinging nettles are not showy or obvious plants. Their flowers are quite small and hang in dangling, branching clusters from the junctures between the leaves and stem. One cluster holds all female flowers and the other all male, and because none of them have petals, the flowers are not the best way to identify nettles. The leaves, too, lack obvious identifying characteristics. They grow opposite each other on the stem, are from oval to elongated-oval in shape, and toothed around the margins—in short, they look like a lot of other leaves. The best way to recognize stinging nettles is by texture rather than by botanical details. The leaves and stems look hairy, and it's the hairs that cause the trouble.

Each hair is a small defense mechanism that will release a pain-causing substance if the tip of the hair is broken off by a passing person or animal. The tip of the hair is actually a bulb, which breaks away quite easily, leaving a stiff, needle-sharp point to puncture the skin. The hair is stiff because it contains silica, and it operates as if it were a miniature hypodermic needle.

The experts don't know the chemical composition of the pain-inducing substance. Some early researchers thought it was formic acid, which is also found in ants, but more recent studies have isolated at least three substances: acetycholine, histamine, and 5-hydroxytryptamine. When these three substances are eliminated from the nettle's fluid, however, the fluid still stings, so there is obviously an additional substance that has not yet been analyzed.

Despite their sting, many uses have been found for nettles. Folk medicine used to prescribe a whipping with nettles for rheumatism or weak muscles. After the initial sting from the first few strokes, the nettles didn't hurt the skin anymore and actually gave some relief from pain in the muscles and joints. You will notice yourself that after an encounter with nettles, you feel a warm, tingling sensation, perhaps indicating increased circulation, where the nettles hit.

Nettles are also edible. Whatever substance it is that causes the pain disappears when nettles are boiled or when they are cut and allowed to dry. Nettles are high in protein, minerals, and vitamins and are therefore a favorite with edible wild-food enthusiasts, who pick the leaves with gloves on and cook them as they would spinach. In some European countries, nettles are harvested and dried as supplementary fodder for cattle, goats, and chickens.

Stinging nettles are perennial and spread each year by

means of creeping underground stems. Where you encounter one, therefore, you are likely to encounter a whole bed. It is to your advantage to learn to identify stinging nettles, both to avoid contracting the seven-minute itch and also, because they are so abundant and persistent, to consider making use of them.

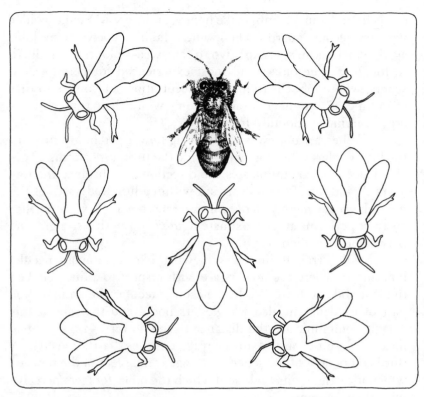

# HONEYBEES
*Learning to Observe an Insect That
Knows Where It's Going*

$B$y late spring, honeybees are all over the place, visiting
the many species of flowers that provide nectar and pollen for
their hives. But they are not foraging at random. The term *beeline*
refers to the relatively straight line that honeybees follow from
their food sources back to their hives. Surprisingly, they fly almost as directly from their hives to their food sources. Honeybee
foragers know where they're going because senior foragers, called
*scouts*, give them directions.

Within each honeybee colony labor is divided by age, the
youngest workers staying home to feed the larvae and take care of
the queen. Young workers also keep the hive clean, construct new

egg cells and honeycomb, make honey, and store it. Slightly older workers become guards. Then, when the honeybees are middle-aged, which means perhaps two to four weeks old, they graduate to foraging. The oldest and most experienced foragers become scouts, whose job it is to locate concentrations of flowers so that the numerous younger foragers won't waste their time and energy searching randomly for food.

When a scout finds a promising flower patch, it returns to the hive to alert other foragers. Inside the hive, it performs a special dance that communicates the direction and distance the foragers should fly. If the flowers are within a hundred yards of the hive, the scout merely dances in a circle, but if they are farther away, it performs an approximate figure eight with a straight line between the two loops.

The straight line is somewhat like a compass needle, pointing to where the flowers are with respect to a line between the sun and the hive. While the scout executes the straight line part of its dance, it also waggles its body, and the rate of this waggle communicates the distance to the flowers—a fast waggle means "close by" and a slower waggle means "farther away." A third component of the scout's message is the scent of the flowers, which it carries on its body and which the other foragers perceive with their antennae.

Some of the colony's scouts use this same dance language when it comes time for an overpopulated honeybee colony to divide and disperse. Whereas most animals disperse by sending out their young, honeybees do just the opposite. It's the old queen, with a mixed-age assortment of about half her workers, who leaves, while the other half of the workers stay to serve the first—or the strongest—of the new young queens, who emerge from pupation a day or so after the old queen departs.

The old queen and her workers are called a *swarm*. As with foraging, instead of the whole swarm searching randomly for a new hive, it's more efficient for the senior scouts to look for something suitable and come back with reports. The swarm waits in a mass attached to the branch of a tree or shrub near the old colony. Sometimes several of the scouts find suitable homes— either hollow trees or a beekeeper's hives—and come back to dance out directions and distances. The energy of each scout's dance communicates the desirability of the find, one scout finally outdancing all the others and persuading the swarm to follow its instructions. The whole swarm then flies at once, creating an impressive display of honeybee multitudes as it moves toward its new home.

All this activity takes place during the warm months, the swarms occurring in late spring or early summer. In the fall, unlike bumblebees and social wasps, who die off, leaving only fertilized queens to start all over again in the spring, honeybee colonies withdraw into their hives, cluster together for warmth, and feed on their stored honey through winter. Individual honeybees—especially those born during the peak of the colony's warm-weather activities—are not especially long-lived, but the colony itself persists year after year by dividing tasks among overlapping generations and depending on its oldest members to scout, communicate, and keep the honeybees we see outside their hives on course.

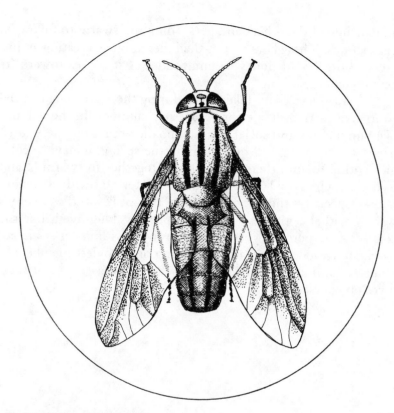

## DEER FLIES
### Learning to Understand Insect Reproduction

$B$lack flies are the earliest of the biting insects to reactivate in the spring, with mosquitoes close behind. When you find yourself being bitten by yet a third blood-hungry insect, there's only one consolation: the beginning of deer-fly season means black-fly season is almost over.

Deer flies are named for their harassment of deer, but they harass human beings and other mammals, too. They look somewhat like houseflies, but they're bigger, their wings are patterned—and they bite. Among the biting flies it's always the females who are the offenders. While their males are off dabbling with flowers, the females must search for a source of warm, red blood to supply the protein they need to produce their eggs.

All the biting flies have specially adapted mouthparts to help them obtain their meals, but each type uses its mouthparts in a slightly different way. Whereas the female black fly is so subtle you don't even feel her while she's biting, and the female mosquito is a bit of a surgeon, making a delicate, pinprick incision, the deer fly rams her sharp jaws right into your skin. Because she's less careful than her cousins and less speedy to fly away when she's discovered, we probably kill more deer flies than black flies or mosquitoes. But there doesn't seem to be any significant difference in their numbers.

If the deer fly obtains her blood meal and escapes unharmed, her next job is to lay eggs on a piece of aquatic vegetation just above the waterline. After she's deposited the black, shiny eggs, which usually happens four to seven days after she's fed, her job is done. She might live on for a few more days, but the adult stage of a deer fly's life cycle isn't nearly as long as the earlier stages.

When the eggs hatch one to three weeks after they're laid, the deer fly larvae drop into the shallow water or muddy soil near the edge of the water. At first they live on yolk stored in their midgut, but within a few days they begin the eating, growing, molting stage of their life cycle. During this stage they perform important services as predators of other insects in the water and mud. They are a key part of the intricate network of checks and balances that operates in aquatic ecosystems.

The deer fly goes through winter as a larva and pupates during the warm days of late spring. It seeks drier soil away from the watery, muddy larval habitat for this inactive stage of its life cycle. After a one-to-three week period of rest and change, the adult deer fly emerges from the soil in late May or early June. The males feed on plants and hover around in large groups waiting for the females, who emerge slightly later than they do. Males don't live as long as females and might die within a few days of mating. The mated females, meanwhile, search for warm-blooded creatures, who will provide them with their necessary meal of blood.

In the western part of the United States, deer flies can

transmit a disease called tularemia when they bite, but in the East they just bite. Learning about an insect's life cycle and seeing how you fit into it may help you accept the seasonal irritations you must suffer, but when the deer flies add their painful bites to those of the black flies and mosquitoes, this knowledge will not necessarily help you feel more benevolent.

# SUDDENLY SUMMER

# DAISIES AND
# BLACK-EYED SUSANS
## Learning to Observe Look-Alike
## Wild Flowers

*A*s roadside flowers color up for their summer performances, two of the most familiar attract attention as apparent variations on the same theme. Is a daisy a white version of the black-eyed Susan, or is a black-eyed Susan a yellow version of the daisy? If you look closely at these two flowers, especially if they happen to be growing conveniently side by side, you will see that they are not the same flower at all.

Both belong to the composite family—their flower heads are composed of numerous individual florets—but the daisy's flower head differs significantly from the black-eyed Susan's.

Starting with the central disk florets, you will notice that the yellow center of the daisy is relatively flat—like a button with an indentation in the middle. The purple-brown center of the black-eyed Susan is thicker and more cone-shaped. The ray florets, which look like petals, also differ in more than just color. The white rays of the daisy are shorter, broader at the tips, and more numerous. The yellow rays of the black-eyed Susan are more loosely spaced and hang slightly downward.

If you look on the underside of the flower heads, you will see that the daisy has a ring of close-growing green bracts that seem to hold the white petals firmly in place. The black-eyed Susan, on the other hand, has long, loose-hanging bracts that fall away from the flower head. They look as if their job was over when the flower opened.

In handling the two plants, you will feel some differences too. The daisy's stem is smooth, pliable, and covered with small, deeply cut leaves that appear lacy. The black-eyed Susan's stem is rough and hairy. It feels coarse to the touch, even a bit brittle. The leaves are bigger, straight around the edges, and feel furry.

With a hand lens, you can carry your investigations a step further. Pull out one of the daisy's rays, and you will see that the base is slightly swollen. That's because the daisy's rays are females, and if they are pollinated, each ray can produce a seed just like the seeds that the small, tightly packed disk florets will produce. If you pull out one of the black-eyed Susan's rays, you will see that the base is straight sided—no room for a seed to develop there. Its rays are infertile. Their only job is to attract insects to pollinate the dark disk florets.

Another difference that you'd need a book to tell you about, or maybe just several years of patient observation, is that the daisy is a *perennial* and the black-eyed Susan is a *biennial*. That means the daisy comes back, flowers, and produces seeds year after year from the same rootstock. Each black-eyed Susan, in contrast, has a two-year life cycle. From seed it takes the plant two years to flower and produce new seeds, and then the whole plant dies.

The reason the two familiar flowers are so different is that they are only distantly related. The daisy is a native of Europe and Asia. It found its way to our meadows and roadsides via the early ships that brought goods packed in hay. Daisies and their seeds were mixed into the packing, and they seem to have found our soils to their liking. Black-eyed Susans are natives of North America, but not of the East. Originally they grew only in the West, but as settlers moved westward, black-eyed Susans began to travel eastward, mixed in with the western clover that was being shipped east.

Although these two wild flowers arrived in New England by two distinctly different routes, they respond to the same growing conditions and therefore frequently grow side by side. They like dry fields, roadsides, and other waste places. The daisies bloom first, but the black-eyed Susans are not far behind. Together they add some of the richest colors to our summer scenery—and remind us that similarity has a lot to teach us about differences.

# VICEROY BUTTERFLIES
*Learning to Observe a Mimic*

*W*hen the viceroys appear, it's summer. These medium-sized, orange and black butterflies are best known as mimics of the monarch butterfly, which is unfortunate because mimicry puts the emphasis on superficial resemblance, ignoring all the viceroy's other adaptations and behaviors. Mimicry of the monarch is indeed an achievement, but it's an achievement that serves only the adult viceroy. Furthermore, it's based on so many if's and maybe's that if resemblance of the monarch were all the viceroy had going for it, it might not last very long.

The value of the viceroy's mimicry is based on the monarch's inedibility. Monarch larvae eat milkweed, ingesting a substance that stays with them through adulthood and causes predators to vomit. The strategy would seem quite clever except that some milkweed species don't contain the poison necessary to make a predator vomit, and each individual predator must taste at least one poisonous orange-and-black butterfly before it learns not to eat them. Because some monarchs aren't poisonous and no viceroys are, and because all predators are young and naive once, a considerable number of orange and black butterflies are consumed before all the predators have learned their lesson.

The ways in which the viceroy is different from the monarch are actually more important to its survival than the one way in which it is the same. For instance, the reason we begin to see viceroys early in June, while the monarchs are still working their way north from Mexico, is that the viceroys spend their winters in the same area where they are born. They winter as partially grown larvae hidden in leaf tubes. When the days shorten in the fall, the late-summer larvae begin to build their hibernacula. Before freezing weather arrives, each larva eats a leaf part way down the midrib, rolls what is left into a tube, secures the leaf to its twig with strands of silk, spins more silk inside the leaf to make it waterproof, crawls inside, and becomes inactive. When the cold days of winter come, the larva produces enough *glycerol*—an insect antifreeze—to keep it from freezing.

The leaves that viceroy larvae use to protect themselves in winter belong to the same trees they feed on during the summer. Viceroys prefer willows and poplars to the monarch's milkweeds. The adults lay their well-camouflaged eggs individually on the very tips of these leaves, and four to eight days later each larva hatches and eats its leaf from tip to stem. It feeds at night, rests on the disappearing leaf's midrib during the day, and proceeds systematically through all the leaves on the twig. At this stage of the viceroy's life cycle, it is a humped, mottled, olive and white caterpillar that resembles a bird dropping more than a monarch caterpillar.

After about four to six weeks of eating, growing, and molting five times—the overwintering larvae merely take an extended break for winter between their second and third molts—the viceroy pupates in a mottled brown chrysalis attached to its food tree. A week to ten days later it emerges as a handsome orange and black adult—with a thin black band cutting across the dark veins of its hind wings to differentiate it from the monarch. It is now ready to sip nectar from flowers, mate, and derive whatever protection it can from looking somewhat like a monarch.

Survival through all the early stages of the viceroy's life

cycle has absolutely nothing to do with looking like a monarch. The story of how adult viceroys came to look so much like adult monarchs when they are so unlike each other in all other ways remains an evolutionary mystery. Viceroys do derive some protection from their mimicry during the crucial period when they are mating and laying eggs, but that mimicry is just one last tactic on top of all the others that keep the species alive.

# RUBY-THROATED HUMMINGBIRDS
## *Learning to Understand Hummingbird Aeronautics*

*I*t's easy to mistake hummingbirds for big insects. They move like insects, and you usually see them sipping nectar from flowers, which is more typical of insects than birds. Hummingbirds have all the standard bird equipment; they have merely evolved different ways of using it in order to take advantage of the food they find hidden deep inside flowers.

Their wings are their most exceptional adaptation. Most birds' wings bend freely at the shoulder, elbow, and wrist, giving them a flapping or soaring flight. The hummingbird's wings are almost rigid. They move mostly at the shoulder, where a swivel joint enables them to tilt first one way, then another to maintain a hovering position.

The wings don't just flap—they make high-speed little figure eights as they beat back and forth so rapidly we hear them as a hum and see them only as a transparent blur. Researchers working with special movie cameras slowed these wingbeats to the speed of a slow-flying gull in order to study the movements in detail. In addition to recording the wings' exact positions as they sculled back and forth, the researchers determined that the hovering hummingbird beats its wings over fifty times a second.

One dedicated researcher calculated that while a hummingbird is hovering, it is expending ten times as much energy as a human being running nine miles per hour. To sustain this level of energy output, the human being would have to eat 285 pounds of hamburger, or its caloric equivalent, each day. The hummingbird does it all on nectar and insects—the sugar in the nectar for the instant energy it needs to stay in motion, and the protein of the insects for growth and tissue repair. Hummingbirds eat about every ten or fifteen minutes, sometimes consuming half their weight in sugar daily.

The hummingbird's bill and tongue are specially adapted to enable these intense little birds to feed from flowers. The shape and length of the bill are related to the particular flowers that the particular species of hummingbird frequents—and, incidentally, pollinates. The ruby-throated hummingbird, the only species that nests in the East, has a needlelike bill just the right length for probing lilacs, fireweeds, jewelweeds, and cardinal flowers.

A hummingbird's tongue is long and can be extended beyond the end of its bill to reach into hidden nectaries. The tongue's outer edges curl inward to create two tubes through which the hummingbird sips nectar. Small brushes at the tip lap up any insects that happen to be inside the flower.

Some ornithologists theorize that the nectar-eating came after the insect-eating. Early in the hummingbird's evolutionary history, the ancestral birds discovered a sweetness inside the flowers they were exploring for insects and incorporated nectar into their diet. The sugar permitted a more energy-expending way of life, and the hummingbird evolved its unique hovering, sipping, pollinating relationship to tropical flowers—and then to flowers much farther north. The brave little ruby-throat migrates over two thousand miles to sip from our northern flowers and nest in New England.

Hummingbirds have to expend a lot of energy to live the way they do, but nothing's wasted. Food is converted to motion, and motion leads to more food-getting, as well as to the courting, mating, nesting, raising of young, and migrating that perpetuate the different species. Hummingbirds operate at intensities that would burn human beings up, but their familiar presence at our brightest flowers proves that for them, at least, high speed works.

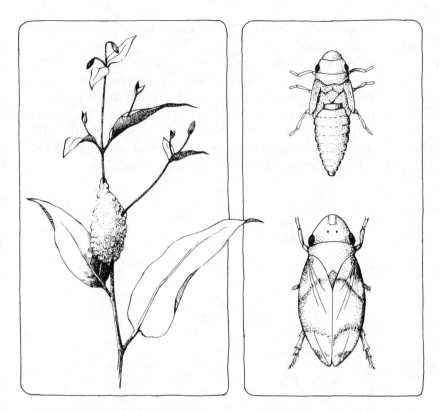

# SPITTLEBUGS
*Learning to Observe a Survival Strategy*

$F$rogs, snakes, spiders, cuckoos, and even human beings have been blamed for the spit that appears on weed and grass stems during the summer. If you can overcome your aversion and look closely at a healthy globule of the stuff, you'll discover the true spit-maker—a small green insect called the spittlebug.

The spittlebug is the youthful stage of an insect which as an adult is called a froghopper. The froghopper is kin to cicadas, aphids, and other plant-sucking insects, all of whom experience an incomplete, three-stage metamorphosis. During the growing stage between the egg and adulthood, the young are called *nymphs*. The froghopper nymph—the spittlebug—doesn't look much like the insect it will become as an adult. The froghopper is a small brown creature that leaps from plant to plant, looking somewhat like a miniature frog, while the spittlebug is pale green and hides within the safety of its self-made spittle.

The spittle is cool, wet, and slippery to the touch. It's full of air bubbles, but it has the consistency of saliva—or egg whites—rather than of foam. The small spittle-maker is well camouflaged against the plant stem, its two tiny brown eyes the only color visible besides green. The nymph's job is to eat, grow, and molt until the adult insect is ready to emerge from the last nymphal skin. As an adult, the insect won't make spit anymore. It will have flying wings and jumping legs to encourage movement, rather than a spit-producing apparatus to encourage staying still. Late in the summer or during the fall, the traveling froghopper will encounter a mate, fertilize or lay eggs, and then die. The eggs will winter over in the plant stem in which the female laid them and hatch into a new generation of spittlebugs in the spring.

Froghoppers are so small and nondescript and jump so readily if disturbed that they're difficult to see, but spittlebugs attract attention to themselves with their spit. This spit is almost unique in the animal kingdom. Only one other insect—a waxmoth caterpillar—produces a similar substance. Spittlebugs manufacture their spit from the plant juices they suck and a waxy ingredient produced by glands in the abdomen. The two mix and are excreted as a clear liquid. Air blown out through a special pumplike structure beneath the abdomen produces bubbles in the liquid one at a time, all of an equal size, eventually creating the frothy appearance of the spit. The spittlebug usually perches head downward on the stem, letting gravity pull the protective spit over its body.

This spit serves the growing spittlebug in several ways. First, it provides it with a way to rid itself of excess plant juices. Inside the mass of spittle, the spittlebug has its beaklike mouth submerged in the plant stem and spends most of its time sucking liquid. Second, the spittle creates a controlled environment—moist and cool—for the young insect to live in while it's growing. This environment is so important to the spittlebug that whenever it moves to a new part of the plant, it immediately—within about five minutes—produces a new spittle mass. Finally, the spittle protects the spittlebug from predators. The spittlebug's only known predator is a species of wasp that recognizes the spit as the home of an insect that will make a good meal for its own young.

If the spittlebug's spit still offends you even after you know what it is, just accept it as a clever way for an insect to protect itself during its flightless youth. Other life forms might have evolved more complex or elaborate survival strategies, but insects seem to have come up with the most surprises.

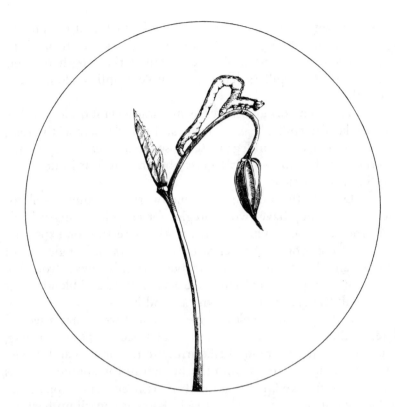

# INCHWORMS
## *Learning to Observe Locomotion*

*P*icnic tables seem to be a favorite measuring place for inchworms. When you spot a small green caterpillar making its way an inch at a time across a table top, observe its method of locomotion. It moves by looping its slender abdomen upward and drawing its hind end up to its front end. Then it stretches its front end a body length forward and starts all over again. Other caterpillars move with a more rippling motion, keeping their entire bodies close to what they're crawling on.

The difference in movement is explained by a difference in legs. The wormlike bodies of caterpillars, which are the immature stages of moths and butterflies—in the case of inchworms, moths—are divided into thirteen segments. Most caterpillars have *true legs* on their first three segments, stubby appendages called *prolegs* on segments six through nine, and a final pair of appendages called *anal prolegs*, or *claspers*, on segment thirteen. With eight pairs of legs and prolegs distributed the length of their bodies, most caterpillars have no trouble rippling along quite smoothly.

The inchworm, however, is missing several prolegs. It has the regular caterpillar legs up front and the claspers at the rear, but only one pair of prolegs to serve segments six through nine. Therefore it has to loop its legless abdomen upward out of the way in order to move.

Despite the missing legs, inchworms do quite well for themselves. They have two strategies for escaping hungry birds and other enemies. When an inchworm is resting or expecting trouble, it holds onto a branch with its claspers and single pair of prolegs and leans the rest of its body rigidly away from the branch at an angle. It looks just like a small twig and blends right in with all the greens and browns around it.

If the predator isn't deceived, the inchworm has a second defense already prepared. When it leaned back to pose as a twig, it attached a single strand of silk firmly to the branch and played out just enough to reach from the branch to the spinneret in its head. If it's attacked, it lets go with its rear end and drops quite suddenly out of the predator's reach. Later it can climb back up its silk lifeline to wherever it was before it was interrupted.

The inchworm's success in escaping its enemies is not always to human advantage. These little caterpillars are not the complete innocents they appear. Two species that cause serious problems are the spring and fall cankerworms. Most inchworms are leaf-eaters, but cankerworms happen to prefer the leaves of trees human beings have planted for fruit or shade.

The life cycles of these two cankerworms are timed to inflict double damage just as the host trees are producing their new spring leaves. The adult moths of the spring cankerworms emerge in the spring, having spent the winter as pupae underground. They mate, lay their eggs, and die, leaving their larvae to hatch and feed on spring foliage. The fall cankerworms, despite their name, get an even earlier start because the adult moths mature in the fall. They mate, lay their eggs, and die before cold weather, leaving the eggs to winter over and hatch early in the spring. These eggs hatch before the spring cankerworm eggs, so the fall cankerworms are already eating leaves when the spring cankerworms join them. These two species working together can severely damage a tree.

But it's hard to think of a solitary inchworm looping across a picnic table as a threat. The small creature works so hard at getting places, it seems as if it might be on an important mission. The Latin name for the inchworm family—Geometridae— suggests one such mission. Perhaps these inch-long caterpillars are geometers, or measurers—an inch at a time—of the earth.

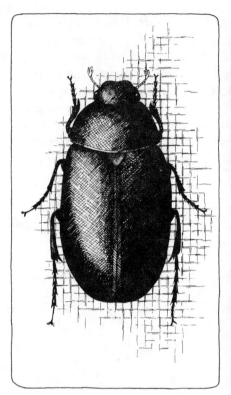

# JUNE BEETLES
## Learning to Observe Metamorphosis

*O*n warm summer evenings, June beetles thud against screened doors and windows. These nocturnal creatures are strongly attracted to light, which explains why they batter themselves repeatedly against screens, sometimes with enough impact to kill themselves. The large brown insects are also known as June bugs, May bugs, and May beetles, reflecting the time of year they are most abundant and some confusion about who they are. If you examine one, you will see the hard, shiny wing covers that distinguish it as a beetle. Its life cycle is also the four-stage, complete metamorphosis of a modern beetle rather than the three-stage, incomplete metamorphosis of the more primitive bug.

Adult June beetles feed mostly on leaves. They have been found on oaks, elms, willows, poplars, hickories, walnuts, ashes, cherries, plums, maples, and beeches. Different species of June beetles prefer different species of trees. The function of these leaf-eaters in the insect's four-stage life cycle is to mate, deposit fifty to one hundred small white eggs in the soil, and die.

The eggs hatch in about two to four weeks, depending on the temperature and moisture of the soil, and the small white grubs, which can become serious agricultural pests during their second year of growth, begin nibbling on the roots of grasses and other vegetation growing nearby. The mother apparently has a good memory of what she liked to eat as a grub, or she recognizes that a freshly plowed and planted field will soon be growing up to grass, farm crops, or a garden, because she deposits her eggs in grain and corn fields, strawberry patches, potato plantings, lawns, and gardens, all of which offer the larvae desirable foods.

The larvae aren't big enough to do much damage their first season, but during the winter they crawl deeper into the soil to hibernate and return the next year with bigger appetites. They become the fat white grubs that are relished by skunks, raccoons, foxes, and moles. At the end of this voracious second season, the grubs hibernate again and return a third season to eat briefly and pupate. The pupa becomes an adult that third season, but the beetle stays underground in its pupal shelter during the winter. The next spring, the adult emerges from the soil, ready to spend its nights feeding on leaves, looking for a mate, and flying against screens.

In natural ecosystems, June beetles are kept in check by the several wild animals who feed on the grubs, by others who feed on adults, and by parasites and diseases. But agriculture has provided such prime and concentrated feeding grounds for their young that June beetle populations have exploded, and they now cause problems for everyone from home gardeners to large-scale farmers. Organic remedies include treating the soil with ashes, watering plants with a burdock mash, or shaking the adults out of trees at night and feeding them to hogs. Other approaches include plowing in the fall to expose the grubs and interrupt their life cycle, leaving an infested field fallow for a year to interrupt the life cycle, or letting hogs and chickens loose in an infested field to root and scratch for the grubs. All these methods are preferable to chemicals, which kill helpful soil dwellers as well as the destructive grubs.

Screens, of course, are not designed to kill insects, but in the case of June beetles they take their toll. For once, a human practice contributes—in a small way—to balancing the interests of human beings and insects rather than, as usual, giving the insects the edge.

# CASSIOPEIA
## *Learning to Enjoy Summer Stargazing*

On a clear, moonless summer night you will see so many stars you might despair of ever learning your way among them. The Big Dipper and Orion are bold enough that they're easy to distinguish, but Cassiopeia, who is described in many star guides as a "straggling W," is easy to find only if you know where she is.

As contrary as it might seem to accomplished stargazers, you should look for Cassiopeia for the first time on a somewhat hazy night. Because she is composed of relatively bright stars—second and third magnitude on a scale that is brightest at zero and invisible to the naked eye beyond six—she, the Big Dipper, and the North Star will be visible, while a lot of the less brilliant stars that might confuse you will be hidden by the haze.

To locate Cassiopeia, start with the Big Dipper. Using the

two stars that represent the front of the dipper as pointers, draw a straight line with your eyes until they encounter a bright, solitary star. This star is the North Star, also called Polaris, because the earth's North Pole points at it. Then move your eyes approximately the same distance beyond the North Star, and look for a large, loose **W**.

If more of us were shepherds or sailors, we wouldn't have any difficulty finding Cassiopeia even on the clearest, starriest of nights, but the habit of staying indoors with our electric lights on has ruined many of us for stargazing. Actually, the earliest stargazers were probably as bewildered as beginners are today—that's why they made up stories about groups of stars to help themselves map the sky. They must have oriented themselves by one familiar star group and then moved their eyes from right to left or up and down to search for other recognizable patterns. After enough consecutive nights with nothing to do but look at the stars, an observer would move among them with the same ease we modern human beings show in negotiating city traffic.

Long before the constellations were fixed into eighty-eight sections of sky by the International Astronomical Union, people had begun naming star groups in honor of gods, heroes, known animals, and imagined beasts. Cassiopeia's story belongs to Greek mythology. She was the wife of the Ethiopian King Cepheus and mother of a lovely young daughter named Andromeda. Unfortunately, Cassiopeia was quite vain, and by boasting that she was more beautiful than the sea nymphs, she incurred their wrath. The sea nymphs appealed to Poseidon, god of the sea, who sent a sea monster against the shores of Ethiopia. The monster, Cetus the Whale, ravaged the coastline and would have destroyed all of Ethiopia, but Cepheus, in response to the advice of an oracle, consented to sacrifice his daughter. He chained Andromeda to a rock where Cetus could find her, but the hero Perseus arrived just in time to slay the whale, save Ethiopia, and win Andromeda's hand in marriage.

All the participants in this drama—Cassiopeia, Cepheus, Andromeda, Cetus, and Perseus—were eventually set close to each other in the heavens, their names providing several star groups with identities, and their stories connecting the constellations in that part of the sky. It would take many nights of deter-

mined stargazing to learn the rest of the constellations that belong
to Cassiopeia's story, but it is enough for a start to locate Cassiopeia herself and learn the five bright stars that belong to her most
uncomfortable-looking chair.

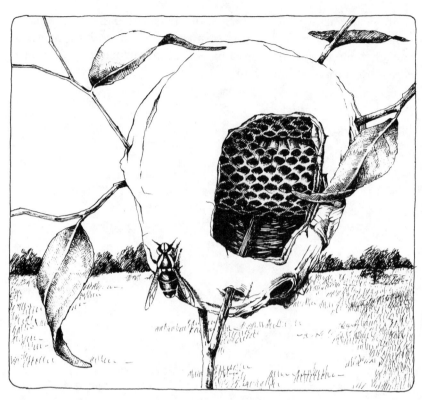

# BALD-FACED HORNETS
## Learning to Observe the Insects of Summer

During the summer, the big gray wasps' nests that dangle from the branches of trees like oversized footballs reach ominous proportions. These nests are constructed by social wasps called bald-faced hornets—"bald" for the white markings on their faces, and "hornets" for their short tempers.

The hornet queens emerge from hibernation early in the spring and begin the hard work of initiating a new colony. First, each queen must build a nest. She creates a strong stalk to hold the nest to a limb, then builds a small structure that looks like a honeycomb to hold her eggs. She then encloses this first stage of her nest within two or three layers of thin gray paper. By early summer the nest is about the size and shape of a chicken's egg.

With a small nest built, the queen turns her attention to raising her first young, who hatch six to eight days after she lays the eggs. She must find fresh insects each day and chew them thoroughly to make a high-protein mash for her offspring. She herself eats liquid foods—nectar, fruit juices, and liquefied insect matter, which is a byproduct of feeding her young. After nine to twelve days, the larvae are ready to pupate. Each one spins a silken cocoon, including a large bubble to cover the entrance to its cell, and ten to thirteen days later emerges as a worker. The workers will help the queen produce a colony that might grow to several hundred individuals during the rest of the summer.

When the queen has some workers to assist her, she becomes a full-time egg-layer. The workers build more egg cells, eventually adding second and third tiers. As the colony grows, the original shelter is no longer big enough, so the workers build new sheaths outside the old. They then cut away some of the innermost layers to make more room inside the nest. By the end of the season, there are always numerous concentric shells with plenty of air space in between to serve as insulation. The completed nest looks like an upside-down cabbage, with fifteen to twenty loosely packed leaves and three or four tiers of egg cells where the cabbage's core should be.

Late in the summer, something signals the workers to shift gears. They build some larger cells and treat the larvae that chance to be developing in these cells with extra care. They feed them more than they feed the other larvae, and in return these special young exude drops of liquid sweeter than the liquid the other young produce. The workers respond by bringing the special young yet more food, and in the process of these mutually reinforcing food exchanges a generation of large, well-fed queens is produced. At about the same time, the old queen lays some unfertilized eggs that receive no special treatment, and these larvae mature into males, whose sole function in this mother-daughter-sister enterprise is to mate with the new queens.

Shortly after the old queen has produced the new queens and males, the tightly knit, highly efficient colony begins to fall apart. The old queen quits laying eggs and dies. The workers begin wandering aimlessly, and some even prey on the larvae of their own colony. Without the queen, the central coordination goes out of the enterprise, and the individuals just bungle around until they die. Many die even before cold weather hits, and those who are still active are killed by fall frosts. The males who mate with the new young queens die shortly after they've mated—only the fertilized queens have the energy and behavioral capacity to hibernate and start all over again in the spring.

It seems somewhat wasteful to spend a whole summer building a huge nest that will never be used again and producing hundreds of individuals who will die at the end of one season. But waste is a human concept. The hornets' objective is to perpetuate their species, and the nest and all the workers are merely what's necessary to transmit the queen's genes.

# BULLFROGS
## *Learning to Observe*
## *a Territorial Amphibian*

*A* midsummer pond resonates with bullfrogs. These large, deep-voiced amphibians sound like a bunch of bagpipes trying to get started as they offer their love songs to the night. The repeated *jug-o-rum*s are the males inviting females to swim by and survey the prospects.

The smaller species of frogs who mate earlier in the spring are what are called *explosive breeders*. They engage in sexual free-for-alls, the fastest and most aggressive males mating with the most females during the few days both sexes are in the breeding ponds. Bullfrogs, in contrast, are more leisurely. They don't even emerge from hibernation until late spring. Then the males battle things out among themselves and establish territories while they're waiting for the females to become ready to lay their eggs. If a male can win a territory with good egg-laying sites, he may succeed in mating with as many as six females in one season.

During the bullfrogs' extended breeding season, the males stay in their territories—or, if one is displaced, he tries to establish another. A male invests most of his energy in establishing and defending his territory, which involves frequent encounters with other males. The resident male will warn another male away, but if the intruder doesn't heed the warning, the two will wrestle until the stronger one dunks the other underwater in a gesture of victory.

Weaker males have two options if they can't wrestle their way into a permanent territory. They can hang around a dominant male's territory in a low-floating, submissive position and try to intercept a female who is approaching the established male. Or they can sing their *jug-o-rums* from temporarily unoccupied territories and dash away if a stronger male approaches. These two options are exercised by younger males, who otherwise wouldn't stand a chance of mating, but neither strategy is as successful as that of having an established territory.

Females stay away from the battling males until they are ready to lay their eggs. Then each female searches for what she perceives as the best egg-laying territory. The bullfrog female is not the least bit coquettish toward the male whose territory she chooses. She swims right up to him and touches him with her head or foreleg. The physical contact signals the male to grab her, and the two drift around in the water together until the female releases her eggs.

Bullfrog eggs float in large rafts on the surface of the water. They hatch in about four or five days, and the tadpoles take care of themselves with no help from either parent. Just as bullfrogs grow bigger than other species of frogs, their tadpoles grow bigger, too. In a cool climate, it takes a bullfrog tadpole two years to transform into an adult. After the transformation, the young bullfrog must grow for another year or two before it is big enough to compete for a territory or to produce eggs.

Bullfrogs, being among the larger members of the aquatic community they belong to, prey on a variety of smaller members, including insects, minnows, crayfish, other frogs, and even smaller members of their own species. In turn, even the biggest bullfrogs are preyed on by bigger predators such as snapping turtles. A summer pond is a busy, competitive, living and dying place, with the bullfrogs' deep-voiced love songs providing appropriate sound effects.

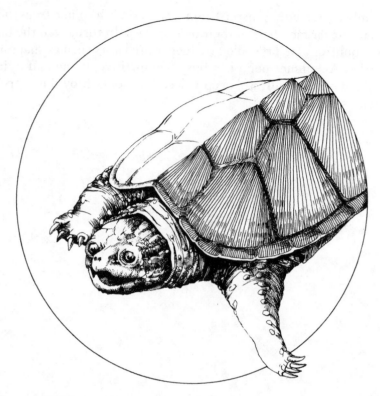

# SNAPPING TURTLES
## *Learning to Observe a Turtle—II*

*I*f turtles could talk, they'd have a lot to tell us. Turtles evolved before the dinosaurs, survived their period of domination, and finally outlived them. These shelled reptiles obviously had an adaptive capacity that the dinosaurs and many other prehistoric reptiles lacked because turtles managed to survive the changes that caused the others to perish. Turtles have also been unusually satisfied with their original design. Once they evolved shells as their distinctive mechanism of survival, over two hundred million years ago, they didn't change much.

Although what makes a turtle a turtle is its shell, various turtles have developed various kinds of shells and various kinds of legs, feet, necks, and mouths for different ways of living. Some turtles live in the oceans, returning to land only to lay their eggs, while others spend their entire lives on dry land. Still others, like the snapping turtle, inhabit freshwater ponds, lakes, marshes, and rivers.

Most turtles are slow-moving and nonthreatening, but the snapping turtle defies this stereotype. Its body isn't especially fast-moving, but its neck and head can move with surprising speed. Even without teeth or venomous fangs, a snapping turtle can inflict a serious wound. All turtles have a horny beak with sharp edges, which they use to tear their food into bite-sized pieces, and if pressed, many turtles will bite in self-defense. The snapping turtle has merely developed a fast and powerful bite into a weapon of offense. The aggressive bite is related to the inadequacy of its shell. The underside of a snapping turtle's shell is much too small to protect its soft body parts, so it compensates by being so vicious that most predators will never even get close to its soft body parts.

When snapping turtles are in water, they are less aggressive than when they're on land. If you stepped on one underwater, it would probably withdraw its head in defense rather than attack your offending foot. It's only on land that the snapper becomes a threat to human toes and fingers. Instructions for turtle handling suggest that you pick up a snapping turtle by its long tail and hold it with its underside toward your leg. That way it snaps angrily at the air, but it can't reach around to bite your legs or hands.

Snapping turtles grow until their shells are about a foot long. Most of them weigh between ten and twenty pounds, but in captivity they can be fattened to over eighty pounds. Once they attain their full size and weight, snapping turtles have few enemies, but when they first hatch—usually two to three months after the eggs are laid—their shells are soft and they're only about an inch long. Snapping turtles hatch snapping, but they're not very threatening because of their diminutive size.

Snapping turtles spend most of their time in water, feeding and mating in their aquatic habitats and hibernating in the mud at the bottom. But the female must leave the water to lay her eggs on dry land. She digs a hole with her hind legs, and after she's laid her eggs, she covers them with soil and debris. She makes no attempt to watch or protect the eggs once she's laid them. Many clutches are destroyed by raccoons, skunks, and other predators who dig them up and eat them.

The snapping turtles who survive their vulnerable early stages and grow to adulthood make important contributions to their aquatic communities. In a large pond, lake, marsh, or river, they serve as population controls on smaller, more prolific animals. They are also scavengers and help keep the water clean by eating animals that die in or near it. Among their few enemies are human beings, who sometimes trap these ancient and well-adapted reptiles to make snapping turtle soup—or merely kill them for fear of their bites, or for the sport of it.

# HERRING GULLS
## *Learning to Observe an Aquatic Bird*

*M*any gulls are "sea" gulls in the sense that they inhabit coastal areas, but that common name is misleading. Many also live inland near freshwater lakes, marshes, and rivers. The herring gull, for instance, which is the species celebrated in *Jonathan Livingston Seagull*, is the commonest gull along the Atlantic coast, but it is also seen around the Great Lakes, along the Mississippi River, and near other bodies of water a considerable distance from the sea.

Herring gulls have been increasing their population and extending their range since the turn of the century. Their recent success can be attributed to laws that made egg-collecting and feather-selling illegal and to the proliferation of garbage dumps around growing urban areas. Ironically, a species that had to be protected in the early 1900s has now, by virtue of its numbers, become a pest in some areas.

Despite the problems herring gulls might be causing human communities, they are important members of the aquatic communities to which they belong. Basically, they are scavengers, feeding on both plant and animal foods, including scraps from human meals, garbage, sewage, and carrion. In places where they can't depend on human excess, they eat small fish, mollusks, crustaceans, other aquatic animals, mice, rats, insects, and even wild berries. As opportunists and general feeders, herring gulls help keep aquatic environments clean.

Herring gulls are well suited for the lives they lead. They can fly high above the water to survey a wide expanse for possible meals. Their long, pointed wings make them skillful soarers and gliders, and they can also cover distances to chase fishing vessels or other boats that might be throwing edible tidbits overboard. Whereas some birds dive from the air into the water after food, the herring gull merely lands and dunks for these surface morsels. It is also clever enough to carry a clam or an oyster into the air and drop it on a rock below to break the hard shell.

The gull's webbed feet serve it both in water and on land. When it's swimming around looking for food, they serve as paddles, and when it's on shore they help it travel over pebbly beaches and soft mudflats. Gulls walk and run quite boldly, with no hint of the duck's ungainly waddle.

In addition to finding a certain amount of their food on the land, gulls also nest on land, laying their eggs right on the ground. Because they are ground nesters, they prefer to nest on islands, where their eggs and young are safe from terrestrial predators.

Herring gulls generally lay three eggs, and both male and female take turns incubating them for the twenty-five to twenty-seven days it takes them to hatch. The parents must be vigilant because herring gulls nest in crowded colonies, and they will eat each other's eggs and young if given the chance. The chicks hatch as well-camouflaged little fluff balls and can walk within a few days, but they stay close to the nest—and their parents' protection—until they can fly. Both parents feed the young by regurgitating food when the young gull pecks at a red spot on the parental beak.

The only problems herring gulls cause within their aquatic communities are to other island nesters. The growing numbers of herring gulls are displacing other species that have always nested on islands. And because herring gulls are aggressive and predatory, even if the other island nesters can still find nesting sites they may lose their eggs and young to these opportunistic gulls. Natural forces would eventually regulate herring gulls if human garbage did not continue to encourage and inflate their numbers. Aquatic communities know how to take care of themselves—if only human communities could figure out what to do with their wastes.

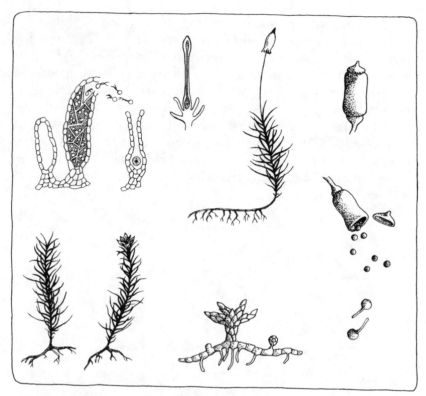

# HAIRY CAP MOSS
## Learning to Look at Moss

On a hot summer day, nothing is quite as soothing as lying down on a cool bed of moss. Mosses are primitive, persistent, and ubiquitous plants. Although they don't advertise themselves with large fronds, showy flowers, or leaves, they are as worthy of attention as ferns, wild flowers, and trees because they are more ancient. Mosses were among the earliest plants to come out of water and find ways to live on dry land.

They evolved tiny rootlike structures to anchor themselves to one spot and self-supporting greenery to manufacture their food. The only thing they didn't evolve is a conducting system, a sophistication that has enabled ferns and flowering plants to grow bigger and in more various habitats. A fully developed conducting system includes roots to carry water from the soil into the plant, a stem to transport materials from the roots to the leaves and back, and veined leaves to specialize in food-making for the whole plant. If you look at a moss plant, you will see that there are no veins to conduct anything anywhere. But even without a conducting system, mosses manage. They hang onto rocks, logs, river banks, and ledges with their little anchors, and they absorb water directly from rain or dew. To cope with dry spells, when more advanced plants draw moisture from deep in the soil, they merely become dormant.

One moss in particular is perfect for lying down on. If it didn't already have a common name, it could easily be called the "mattress moss" because it grows in thick, spongy beds on the forest floor. It's called the hairy cap moss, not for any special hairiness, but for the miniature hairy cap that covers its spores. The spores grow in a small capsule at the top of a slender stalk that rises above the green moss plant. If you find a bed of hairy cap moss with its reproductive structures still intact, you can remove one of the little caps to see for yourself why the moss has been given its name.

After the hairy cap moss sheds it spores, the plant has to go through two stages before a new generation of mosses will produce a new batch of spores. First the spore has to germinate and grow into a small bed of the familiar green moss plants. Some spores produce male plants, and others produce females. You can tell the difference by looking at the tips of the mosses you're lying on. The males have a cup-shaped rosette at their tips, whereas the mature females bear the tall hairy-capped spore stalks.

Before the spore stalk can grow, however, the green moss plant must move into the second stage of its life cycle. A male sperm has to ride a splashing raindrop or swim through a film of water to the egg at the tip of the female plant. Only when the egg is fertilized can it grow into the tall spore stalk that will produce new spores. While most plants show only the spore-producing phase of their life cycle, mosses offer both stages in plain view.

In addition to being among the pioneer plants that moved from water onto dry land, mosses are also among the pioneer plants that repopulate areas denuded by glaciers, forest fires, volcanoes, and other natural disasters. Their spores can travel great distances with the wind, and they can germinate, grow, and reproduce in conditions that would be inhospitable to higher plants. And once they've gotten started, their living and dying adds organic matter to rock particles and gradually creates the soil that will invite other plants to grow.

A moss's role as comforter to overheated human beings has little to do with its evolutionary history. But if in lying on it we learn to value it, it may have a lot to do with both of our evolutionary futures.

# PEPPERMINT
## *Learning to Observe an Edible Plant—I*

*P*eppermint thrives in wet places. It grows in roadside ditches, along brooks, and in marshy meadows, producing its small purple flowers in the heat of summer. Peppermint is fairly easy to identify because it has a purple stem that contrasts with its dark green leaves. To determine whether a particular purple-stemmed plant is a mint, look closely at the stem. If the plant is a mint, the stem will be square. And to determine whether your square-stemmed mint is a peppermint, taste a leaf. As its name implies, the leaf will at first taste hot like pepper and then cool like a mint.

The peppermint that grows wild in this country is not a native. It was first planted here by the English colonists, who valued it as a flavoring and also as a home remedy for such ailments as stomachaches, cramps, diarrhea, colds, and flu. The peppermint they brought was not a native of England either. It was a hybrid of two European mints—one called water mint and the other spearmint, which you might also find growing wild. Spearmint differs from peppermint by having lighter green, more wrinkled leaves. These leaves grow directly from the stem rather than on little stalks, as do peppermint leaves, and they taste altogether milder.

The commercial peppermint fields of Michigan, Indiana, and the Pacific Northwest are another source of the peppermint that now grows wild around this country. This peppermint is grown on a much larger scale than the colonists grew it—and for different purposes. It is harvested for its oil, which is used in gums, candies, toothpastes, soaps, perfumes, and liqueurs.

Although the peppermint you find growing outside herb gardens and commercial fields is an escaped hybrid that has traveled from Europe to the British Isles to North America, it has not changed its appearance or habits upon going wild. Because it is a hybrid, it isn't very good at cross-pollinating and producing viable seeds, so it reproduces itself mostly by sending out underground runners that sprout genetically identical plants. These runners radiate in all directions and break quite easily, with each fragment capable of producing a whole new plant. Once a peppermint gets started, it sends out a new set of runners and produces a new set of genetically identical plants year after year.

If you find peppermint growing close to where you live, you will be able to put it to many uses. Fresh mint leaves can be added to salads, sauces, soups, stews, and casseroles, or stood up—stem and all—in mint juleps or iced teas. You might want to harvest some leaves and dry them for winter use. The best time to do so is just before the plants produce their flowers. The dried leaves can be used in many of the same ways the fresh leaves are used, and they can also be steeped in hot water to make an herb tea.

The use of peppermint as both a flavoring and an herbal medicine goes back at least to the ancient Egyptians and perhaps further. Wherever this hybrid finds wet soil, it's hardy and prolific, so it can easily afford to donate a few of its leaves for human consumption. The peppermint we find growing wild may not be a native plant, but it's certainly a welcome immigrant.

# MILKWEED
## *Learning to Observe a Successful Weed*

Our wild, native milkweeds contribute a powerful fragrance to hot summer days. Their flowers turn weedy fields purplish as they open and invite insects to pollinate them. Few forces interrupt a milkweed's progress—unless a diligent gardener pulls up a persistent shoot, only to discover that the deeply buried rootstock will send up yet another, or the highway crew faithfully mows the milkweeds growing along the roadside, only to find them back again next time they mow.

The perennial rootstock, which is buried below plow level, impossible to pull up by hand, and capable of spreading a little more each year, is only one reason milkweed is so abundant. Another is its effective method of pollination. Insects visit milkweed flowers to sip their nectar, but sometimes, when one lands to enjoy a meal, it gets a leg caught in a tight little trap. The flower surface is slippery and designed to make the insect's leg slide right into a hole where two pollen sacs are hidden. If the insect manages to struggle free, it has the pollen sacs attached to its leg, and the next milkweed it visits receives the pollen. Some insects are not strong enough to free themselves, however, and if you look closely at several milkweed flowers, you are likely to see some of these victims of the milkweed's unusual method of pollination.

The milkweed's method of seed dispersal is yet another component of its success. If you've ever seen a newly opened milkweed pod, you've seen how many seeds each plant produces. But if they all fell to the ground beneath the parent plant, the competition would be too great for very many of them to survive. Therefore each seed has its own silken wings that enable it to travel with the wind. There's still quite a bit of chance involved in where the seeds might land, but that's why there are so many of them. At least some will find dry, sunny locations where new milkweeds can grow.

It's surprising that milkweed hasn't been domesticated by home gardeners. It is edible in almost every stage of its growth and makes an excellent supplement to common garden vegetables. When it first comes up in the spring, its shoots serve as an asparagus substitute. They can be harvested and cooked just like asparagus. When the shoots grow taller, the tender tops can still be eaten. Shortly afterward, the flowers begin to develop, and while they're still in tight green buds, they can be cooked like broccoli. Later, the open flowers can be picked, boiled briefly, then dipped in an egg batter and fried. After the flowers go by, the young seed pods are edible. They should be small and hard when you pick them, because if they're spongy the inedible silk is beginning to develop. The milky white latex that gives milkweed its name is quite bitter, but boiling removes the bitterness. If you boil your milkweed in several waters, you can make it as mild and tasty as any garden vegetable.

Whether or not human beings ever decide to make better use of milkweed, wildlife has been making good use of it all along. Many insects feed on its leaves or its nectar. Hummingbirds, too, compete with insects for the sweet nectar, bypassing the pollinating mechanism because they never land. Another bird, the northern oriole, doesn't use milkweed or its insect associates as a food source, but values the fibers in the milkweed's stem. It uses these fibers to strengthen its hanging nest.

If we are ever reduced to survival foods, perhaps milkweed will come into its own. In the meanwhile, we can revel in its profusion, enjoying the fragrance its numerous flowers add to hot summer days.

# HIGH SUMMER
## AND FALL AGAIN

# MOURNING DOVES
## Learning to Observe Nesting Habits

$S$ummer turns a corner sometime in July. A vague feeling hovers around in the atmosphere until it finally settles in as melancholy. The heat contributes. So do the insects and the sudden burden of vegetables waiting in the garden. If one sound symbolizes this melancholy—enhances it, deepens it, makes it seem atmospheric rather than personal—it's the distant cooing of a mourning dove.

Mourning doves are, of course, not the least bit sad. The male is merely reminding other males of his territorial boundaries, or singing to his mate—*oooah coo coo coo*—as they are working through a second brood. Mourning doves begin preparing for their first brood in April. The male establishes a territory near a good supply of weed seeds and invites a female to join him.

Once an initial pair-bond has been established, which sometimes occurs on the wintering grounds, the two birds remain mated for life. They might join a group of other doves for migration and wintering, but come spring, each pair goes off by itself again.

The male mourning dove participates quite fully in the responsibilities of parenthood. He chooses and defends the territory, selects the nesting site, and brings the female twigs. The female arranges the twigs around and underneath herself, creating a somewhat flimsy platform. If she abandons her nest-building, the male pursues her and drives her back to her task. Her somewhat casual construction project takes place on a horizontal branch—preferably that of an evergreen—about ten to twenty-five feet from the ground. Sometimes the female builds on top of another bird's nest, which provides extra support and stability for her platform. When the nest is finished, she lays two eggs and for the next two weeks takes her turn incubating during the night, while the male incubates during the day.

The males of many species of birds assist in feeding their young, but the males of the pigeon family, to which mourning doves belong, have an unusual relationship to the process. While the pair has been taking turns incubating their eggs, both sexes have been generating pigeon's milk in their crops. This milklike substance provides all the nutrients the hatchlings need for the first few days of their lives. Gradually, the parents introduce seeds into the diet, until after about ten days, the pigeon's milk has run out and the young doves have adjusted to an adult diet.

The young leave the nest after about twelve days, but the parents continue to care for them for a while longer. Then they become busy with a second brood. In the North, mourning doves stop after two broods, but farther south they might produce three, four, or even five. The mortality rate for young doves is high—seventy to eighty percent the first year—but those who survive the first year stand a fair chance of becoming parents to numerous broods themselves.

Mourning dove populations are currently healthy all over the United States because the species has responded positively to human presence. Their preferred habitats are the edges between forests and fields that human beings create wherever they go. The forests provide nesting and roosting sites, and the fields—whether they are cultivated farm fields or merely pastures—provide food. Doves subsist mainly on weed seeds, supplementing these in the fall with whatever grains and corn kernels they can glean from harvested fields.

Human beings named mourning doves for the mournful quality of their song, but it's only at the height of summer that they seem to be mourning something specific. In July, they seem to reflect our sense of melancholy as summer travels toward fall.

# CARDINALS
## Learning to Observe a Bird Who Is Expanding Its Range

So much of our observation of the natural world has been preempted by scientists and researchers that it's nice to have a few species doing things that make the professionals dependent upon amateur observers. The cardinal is just such a species. This bright red, crested bird, which has always been familiar in the South, is now expanding its range northward. To keep track of its progress, researchers are asking northern observers to report sightings in new areas and increases in numbers where the birds have already been seen.

The story that's unfolding with the help of field observations from the northern Midwest, New England, and southern

Canada began around the turn of the century, and it's still in progress. Records from the Midwest and Canada indicate that the cardinals began to increase their population in Michigan around 1900 and first nested in Ontario in 1901.

The invasion of New England occurred a little later. During the 1940s cardinals increased their numbers in northern New Jersey and began working their way up the Hudson and Connecticut River Valleys into southern New England. They first nested in Connecticut in 1943, showed up in Massachusetts in considerable numbers during the fall of 1957, and reached Vermont by the early 1960s.

With cardinals continuing northward year by year, researchers have had to revise their early speculation that the range expansion would be stopped by snow, harsh climate, and evergreen forests. It seems now that the theorists will have to wait patiently until the rest of the evidence is in.

The causes of the cardinal's range expansion are not clearly understood. Other species of birds are also headed northward—the tufted titmouse, the mockingbird, and the Carolina wren. But each of these species has different food and habitat requirements, different relationships to human communities, and different sensitivities to climate. Perhaps when the ranges of all four species have finally settled, researchers will be able to explain what each of the species has been doing and why.

In the meanwhile, hypothetical reasons for the cardinals' expansion include the perhaps warming climate, the improving cardinal habitat as abandoned farms have grown back to brush and new forest, the planting of ornamental shrubbery around houses, towns, and parks, and the massive offering of birdseed at feeders. These improved living conditions have resulted in larger populations of cardinals, which in turn have produced the pressure to expand. Cardinals do not migrate or even travel very far as adults, but the young wander after nesting season and throughout the winter. These young birds tend to follow river valleys in their explorations, and many have drifted northward in their search for unoccupied territories. Because cardinals are very flexible in their choices of nesting habitat and food, the wandering young have adapted readily to their new environments.

What makes the cardinal's progress interesting to scientists and casual observers alike is that it's happening obviously and measurably, even if the researchers don't know yet exactly why. The cardinal's range expansion offers even the most inexperienced and tentative of observers a chance to learn something—and perhaps to discover something—about the species. No one will ever have the chance to be another Audubon, wandering through virgin territories where everything is unknown, but the cardinal's invasion of new areas offers today's observers a touch of the old excitement that early naturalists must have felt when they witnessed something for the first time.

# SKUNKS
## Learning to Understand a Skunk

*R*ecords kept during a six-month period in Ohio show skunks to be high on the list of road kills, with only rabbits and opossums accounting for more bodies. Why so many dead skunks? It's all because of those famous—or infamous—scent glands.

Somewhere back in evolutionary history, the skunk discovered that scent glands could be used as defensive weapons. Other members of the skunk's family—weasels, otters, minks, fishers, and martens—have similar glands, but they use their scents only in mating and establishing territory. For defense, they depend on other adaptations, such as speed and agility. While these other animals have developed long slender bodies well suited to attack and escape, skunks have developed fat, slow-moving bodies well suited to standing still.

A skunk's experience teaches it that it does not have to run from anything. Most wild animals learn at an early age that skunks are not to be tangled with, so most skunks lead relatively unthreatened lives with only an occasional need to strike ominous poses. A skunk is so sure of itself that it goes through a whole set of rituals before it resorts to its ultimate weapon. First, it stamps its feet to announce that it's nervous. If that's not enough to discourage an animal who has come too close, the skunk raises its tail as further warning. As long as the tip of the tail is still hanging downward, there is still time for the other animal to retreat. But if the animal is either too young or too foolhardy to read the message and leave, the tip of the tail shoots up and the skunk lets loose with its spray.

The spray is a fine mist that can hit a chosen target up to about ten feet away. The target is usually an animal's face and eyes. A chemical agent in the spray burns the animal's eyes and mucous membranes and temporarily blinds it. The pain and smell are powerful enough to impress most animals for a lifetime. The mere sight of black and white fur is enough to prevent them from ever attacking again. The skunk's experience with animals has therefore given it a sense of invulnerability.

This sense of invulnerability creates a problem when it comes to cars. To a skunk, an oncoming car is just another threat to be dealt with as all other threats have been dealt with. But the skunk doesn't have time even to strike an ominous pose before the car hits. The rest of the story is told by the number of dead skunks you see along the roads.

A related question is: What are skunks doing around roads in the first place? The answer has to do with food. Skunks are opportunistic carnivores. They like insects, mice, bird and turtle eggs, toads, frogs, and just about anything else they can find that doesn't require much of a chase. They also like carrion, or dead flesh. In their nocturnal foraging, they may catch a whiff of a road kill and be in the process of eating an easy meal when they themselves become the next statistic.

It will be interesting to see how skunks as a species will react to the relatively recent development of cars. All their instincts tell them to stand their ground, which is a suicidal way of dealing with this new threat. The car-skunk issue raises the question of whether a species with instincts that function successfully in the natural world can survive a new enemy that does not respond as natural predators do.

In the meanwhile, it is we who drive the cars who are the losers. A dead skunk means more than just an unpleasant smell. It also means one less appetite out there searching for a meal of insects, mice, and other high-population pests. If the car is currently winning, we are currently losing, and the only question yet to be answered is whether the skunk or the car will be the ultimate survivor of this period of evolutionary history.

# INDIAN PIPES
## *Learning to Observe an Unusual Flower*

$M$ost woodland wild flowers blossom while they can still get some sun—in the early spring before the trees leaf out. But one of the most unusual species doesn't appear until mid-summer. As it pushes up through the leaf litter in the deep shade under oaks or evergreens, it looks like a waxen white sculpture of a flower. It's called an Indian pipe.

You might not even recognize the Indian pipe as a flowering plant. The flower itself, which hangs like a small bell from the top of the stem, is shaped like a small flower—or, as its common name suggests, like a small pipe bowl—but the petals lack color. Its stem is white too, and so are the little scales that represent the leaves. Furthermore, if you touch an Indian pipe, it doesn't feel like a flower. It feels cold and clammy—more like a mushroom.

This strange but beautiful little plant in some ways resembles mushrooms. It lacks chlorophyll and therefore cannot manufacture its own food. But rather than obtaining the food it needs from dead and decomposing matter as mushrooms do, the Indian pipe obtains its food indirectly from the roots of neighboring trees.

The tree roots and Indian pipe roots become intermeshed with each other and with a species of fungus that occurs naturally in woodland soils. In the case of the tree, the fungus absorbs food from its photosynthesizing host and, in return, helps the tree absorb minerals from the soil. In the case of the Indian pipe, however, the fungus acts more like a bridge. It passes food it has absorbed from the tree along to the Indian pipe, and, in return, passes minerals from the Indian pipe back to the tree. The only benefit the fungus derives from the Indian pipe is a substance that stimulates it to grow. The Indian pipe is a very dependent third partner in the tree-fungus relationship—the tree and the fungus can function quite happily without the Indian pipe, but the Indian pipe cannot even begin to grow without the fungus that will connect its roots to the roots of a nearby tree.

Although the Indian pipe feeds itself in this indirect, unflowerlike way, it reproduces itself just like a flower. If you look closely at the delicate white flower that hangs from the top of the white stem, you will see four or five petals, eight to ten pollen-laden male parts, and a five-sectioned female part. After pollination, the flower swells into a many-seeded capsule and stands erect. Eventually, the seed capsule breaks open, spilling its contents to the forest floor, where new Indian pipes can grow in close association with the fungus that the germinating seeds will encounter in the soil.

An Indian pipe is a prime example of an organism that belongs exactly where it is. It refuses to cooperate with anyone who might want to take it anywhere else. If you pick it, it will turn black. If you try to transplant it or grow it from seed, it won't survive because it needs both its special root fungus and also its neighboring trees. In every way the Indian pipe is a stubborn—if dependent—individualist. Defying both cultivation and easy categorization, it grows quietly in the moist, sunless soils of oak and evergreen woods. If you want to see an Indian pipe, therefore, you will have to find one growing and observe it where it lives.

# THISTLES
## *Learning to Observe Plant Anatomy—I*

*I*t's easy to think of wild flowers as gentle, ethereal things—fragile stems topped with colorful flowers and soft, cool leaves, soothing to the touch. Well, the thistle is different. The common bull thistle, which grows in pastures and along roadsides throughout the East, has sharp spines all over it—on the stem, on the leaves, and even on the green bracts that clasp the pinkish-purple flowers. And these spines won't fold beneath your fingers. Nor can you find a space big enough between any two of them to place a cautious finger and thumb to break the stem. If you try to pick the thistle anyway, the spines will draw blood.

If the thistle is growing in a pasture, the spines explain why it hasn't been eaten by the cows, sheep, or even goats. As much as these spines hurt human fingers, they would more cruelly lacerate the inside of an animal's mouth. The only part of the thistle that's approachable is the flower itself, which is soft and sweet-smelling. The flowers want to be touched, especially by insects, in order to be pollinated. Bees and butterflies are frequent visitors, and hungry hummingbirds stop by occasionally, too. Later in the growing season, when the seeds have matured into protein-rich morsels and the white down hidden inside the spiny green bracts has begun to expand, goldfinches visit thistles for food and nesting material. They eat as many seeds as they can find and line their nests with the soft white down.

A thistle's main business, however, is not to feed wildlife but to reproduce itself. The spines, flowers, and, later, the down, are all parts of its reproductive strategy. While the spines save the plant from being picked or eaten before it's had a chance to produce its flowers, and the bright, scented flowers attract insect pollinators, the construction of the flowers guarantees a high rate of pollination. All that purple fringe is actually the tips of numerous, tightly packed, tubular flowers. The thistle is a composite—like the daisy, black-eyed Susan, and aster—but it lacks the ray florets. Its flower head is composed completely of disk florets.

These disk florets produce their pollen first, pushing it up on the tips of their emerging female parts. Insects pick up this exposed pollen as they sip nectar. After the pollen has been carried off by insects or become inactive, the female flower parts open to receive pollen from other thistles. Each floret is a complete flower and can produce a seed if an insect pollinates it. As an assurance that at least some of the seeds will find suitable places to germinate and grow into new plants, all of the seeds are equipped with special thistledown. Milkweed seeds have similar down to help them fly, but thistledown is branched and featherlike. It can carry the seed long distances on even the gentlest breeze.

Most thistles are biennial. The first year, the seeds germinate and produce a taproot and a rosette of spiny green leaves. The second year, the plant flowers, produces seeds, disperses them, and then dies. One species—the Canada thistle—produces a perennial rootstock, which makes it a more serious pest than other thistles. The rootstock grows longer each year, sending up more and more thistles. A farmer who tries to destroy it with a cultivator merely chops the rootstock into small sections, and each small section develops into a new plant.

Thistles are attractive when they are in bloom, and if you see one from a distance, it's certainly worth approaching for a closer look. Thistles will never make it into bouquets or gardens, but their adaptations assure them a place wherever else they grow.

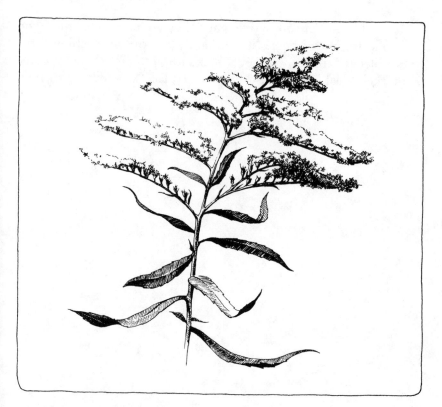

# GOLDENRODS
## *Learning to Observe Plant Anatomy—II*

Goldenrods are sobering. When they appear, it's time to admit that you're not going to get to all your summer projects. These late bloomers are among our most familiar wild flowers, but the goldenrod's general appearance is much better known than the structure of its individual flowers. It takes a hand lens to see the structure, and even with a hand lens, the details are difficult to perceive.

The overall impression a goldenrod gives from a distance is that of a lot of yellow at the top of a tall green stem. When you approach the goldenrod and look closely at the yellow, you will see that it is composed of numerous small tufts. Each little tuft is a separate unit, clasped at the base by a green, cuplike structure.

If you isolate one of these tufts and examine it with your

naked eyes, you might be able to distinguish two different shapes among the yellow bristles. Around the outside, the bristles look like fringe, while toward the center they look more like clubs. With a hand lens you can see the differences more clearly, and with a hand lens plus a good imagination you might be able to see a similarity between the goldenrod's miniature arrangement and the more visible arrangement of a daisy.

Goldenrods—like daisies, black-eyed Susans, asters, and thistles—are composites. Each little yellow tuft is a densely packed flower head composed of a few tubular disk florets surrounded by several flat rays. In goldenrods, both disks and rays are fertile, so all that get pollinated will produce seeds. After the yellow flowers have gone by, goldenrods are adorned by fuzzy little seed heads that last well into winter.

Most composites have large, inviting flower heads that insects can see with no trouble, but a goldenrod has a slightly different strategy. Its array of small flower heads, which are clustered at the top of the plant, presents passing insects with a mass of yellow. An insect who stops to explore discovers that it has its choice of nectar from thousands of individual florets arranged in hundreds of little flower heads, all right next to each other on a single plant.

Goldenrods are popular with insects, attracting honeybees, bumblebees, butterflies, several beetles, and at least one species of fly. Anyone who thinks goldenrods cause hay fever should sit next to one and observe the number of insect pollinators who visit it. Insect-pollinated plants don't send much pollen into the atmosphere and therefore don't contribute significantly to human allergies. The real culprits are the wind-pollinated flowers that bloom less visibly nearby. The reason goldenrods get so much blame is that they bloom abundantly, attracting everyone's attention, at the same time the wind-pollinated ragweeds produce their small flowers. It's these hardly noticeable ragweeds that cause the worst of the late-summer allergies.

Many of the most familiar wild flowers of our fields and roadsides are foreigners, but goldenrods are natives. They thrive in open, sunny, unattended areas, multiplying by means of both seeds and underground runners. Over one hundred species of goldenrods can be found in the United States, many of them difficult even for botanists to distinguish. To make identification more complicated, some of the species hybridize. Botanists use the basic shape of the flowery top and the veining of the leaves to tell goldenrods apart, but all goldenrods have one thing in common—the profusion of small golden flowers that give them their name.

# WOLVES
## *Learning to Observe an Inheritance in Our Pet Dogs*

*M*ost of us will never see a live, wild wolf, but we can see remnants of their habits and behavior in domestic dogs. Until the 1960s many experts thought domestic dogs were descended from two different wild canines: some breeds from the golden jackal and others from the wolf. But now researchers have eliminated the golden jackal, leaving the wolf as the common ancestor of all our modern breeds.

Wolves are carnivores, with the teeth to seize, tear, crush, and nibble flesh. Unlike most other carnivores, however, wolves are also coursers, with the skeleton and stamina to chase prey at high speeds over long distances. They are also social, having discovered early in their evolutionary history that they could take down prey much larger than themselves if they cooperated as a pack.

Their ability to find food in any habitat except tropical rain forest or desert enabled early wolves to prosper throughout a vast range. Before human beings began eliminating them and driving the survivors into what is left of the wilderness, wolves lived all over Europe, Asia, and North America. Northern packs fed on caribou, musk ox, and reindeer, while more southerly packs fed on moose, elk, wild sheep, deer, and bison. All of them supplemented their diets with local hares, rabbits, rodents, ground birds, and carrion.

While pack life made the hunting of large hoofed mammals possible, vast tracts of undisturbed vegetation were available to support many herds of such mammals. For a long time, the vegetation, the herbivorous prey species, and the carnivorous predators kept each other in balance, with the wolf packs regulating their own populations in response to the size of the herds they were preying on.

But then, about ten thousand years ago, wolves found themselves in direct competition with another group of accomplished predators—human beings. The wolves' habit of preying on animals that human beings wanted to hunt for themselves—or on animals human communities were raising for domestic consumption—brought the two species into open conflict. While most wolves learned to keep their distance from human beings, some individuals took a different tack. They began to "hang around," and by a process that will probably never be completely understood, they became domestic pets.

The social behavior that makes wolves such successful group predators also made them capable of behaving socially among human beings. In order to live together in a pack, wolves must extinguish a lot of selfish behavior. Young wolves must learn to respect authority, and older, more powerful wolves must learn to exercise restraint. Food must be shared, the young of one dominant pair must be protected and cared for by the entire pack, and all the individuals in the pack must understand and respond to each other's statuses and signals in appropriate ways.

The wolves who began to associate with human beings must have recognized that we were not wolves, but our social interactions were familiar enough to them that they felt at home within human families, or "packs." The wolves who went domestic sacrificed the right ever to become pack leaders, but in return they receive a share of human food.

Ten thousand years later, our domestic dogs have been bred so far away from their wolf ancestors that many of them have no physical resemblance to the wolf whatsoever. But underneath those various doggy exteriors are social tendencies carried by wild wolf genes.

# EASTERN COYOTES
## *Learning to Understand Animal Demographics*

*W*hile your chances of seeing a wild wolf are decreasing, your chances of seeing a wild coyote are increasing. At about the same time that human beings were killing off North American wolves and driving them further into the wilderness, coyotes were beginning to extend their range. Originally they inhabited the prairies and brushy, wooded areas of the West, venturing only as far east as Michigan. But from Michigan, they gradually traveled north of the Great Lakes through Ontario to the St. Lawrence River Valley. From these northern locations they have moved southward into New York State, New England, and even

New Jersey. By the 1940s coyotes were established in the East, but Easterners were not sure exactly who or what they were.

Some people thought these new animals were wolves. A coyote does look somewhat like a wolf, but it is smaller, its nose is narrower—more like a fox's—and it holds its tail down instead of straight out like a wolf. Other people thought the new animals were only wild dogs, but a coyote's tail is much bushier than a domestic dog's, and a domestic dog's tail is usually curled or sickle-shaped. Still others thought they were crosses between dogs and wolves or between dogs and coyotes. Rumors, theories, tall tales, and look-alikes confused matters until biologists finally began identifying animals that were definitely coyotes. The coyotes were bigger than their western relatives, but they were distinctly different from wolves, domestic dogs, or hybrids of any combination.

Although these new canines were clearly coyotes, there was still some question about their relationship to the western coyote. During the 1960s, two New Hampshire researchers conducted thorough studies of the animal that had established a population in their state. With the help of zoologists at the Museum of Comparative Zoology at Harvard, they identified it as a variant, or subspecies, of the western coyote. Its skull shows evidence of both dogs and wolves in its ancestry, but they are far enough back that this eastern coyote—*Canis latrans variant*—now breeds true. When two eastern coyotes mate, they produce a litter of eastern coyotes rather than an assortment of wolf, dog, and coyote hybrids.

Coyotes can still interbreed with domestic dogs—and sometimes do—but these hybrid coydogs are not genetic participants in the eastern coyote's progress. They are essentially dead ends because they don't inherit the right behavior patterns or physiology to produce successful offspring. A male coydog, for instance, doesn't stay with his female as a male coyote does. Without his help, a female coyote doesn't stand a very good chance of raising her young. A female coydog has worse problems. She comes into heat earlier than coyotes, and therefore, if she finds a mate, she bears her young in the dead of winter, when food is scarce and cold weather is a threat to them. Furthermore, wild coyotes mate with domestic dogs only when other coyotes aren't available, and now that coyotes have established a substantial population of their own kind, domestic dogs are less appealing to them.

Some Easterners are unhappy at the presence of these newcomers, but the coyote wouldn't be here if there weren't a place for them in the changing ecology. As human beings have altered the landscape from forest to cleared land, and then let it return to a mixture of open, wooded, and transitional spaces, animal populations have had to shift and find new balances in response. Eastern coyotes are merely adventurous Westerners who have found the East to their liking.

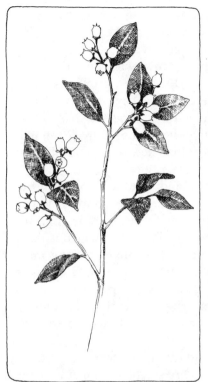 

# BLUEBERRIES
## Learning to Observe an Edible Plant—II

*B*lueberries are natives of North America, and until early in this century they were strictly a wild food. Indians ate them both raw and cooked and may even have burned good blueberry patches to keep them in production. Early settlers picked blueberries to make muffins, pies, and preserves. In some areas wild blueberries are still abundant enough to be harvested commercially, but many of the blueberries sold at grocery stores today are specially bred and cultivated varieties.

The wild species grow in two different ways. Some grow close to the ground in ankle-high thickets, while others grow as medium-sized shrubs. The ankle-high blueberries, which are called *lowbush*, grow in dry, shallow, acid soils. Some of them thrive high up on exposed mountaintops, while others choose open woods or vast sunny fields known as "blueberry barrens." Lowbush blueberries spread by underground stems, called rhizomes, expanding their colonies a bit each year.

*Highbush* blueberries, which grow wild but have also been developed into several cultivated varieties, grow more like small trees, attaining heights of fifteen feet. They prefer wet, acid soils, frequently locating themselves on hummocks in swamps and bogs. Highbush blueberries, like the lowbush, are perennial, but instead of producing spreading rhizomes, they send up new shoots each year from a central crown.

The flowers of both lowbush and highbush species grow in groups at the tips of twigs. They are bell-like, hanging downward to protect their pollen and nectar from exposure to wind and weather. Bees probe each flower for its nectar, which is deep inside the bell. The flower's female part is taller than the male parts, so the visiting bee brushes against her first and deposits some of the pollen it's already carrying as it begins its search for nectar. While the insect is maneuvering, it brushes the shorter male parts and picks up some of their pollen to carry to another flower.

Blueberry flowers can be and often are fertilized by their own pollen, but the resulting berries are smaller and mature later than berries that result from cross-pollination. Each little blue fruit, which is classified as a true berry because a fleshy pulp surrounds a number of seeds, is part of the blueberry plant's strategy to disperse itself. Hungry animals will eat the fruits and deliver the seeds to new locations in their droppings. Fruit-eating birds, such as grouse, scarlet tanagers, bluebirds, robins, and thrushes, are major agents of blueberry dispersal. Bears, foxes, raccoons, skunks, deer, rabbits, chipmunks, and mice also contribute. Blueberry seeds are so small that you don't even notice them as you eat them. But if you pick what looks like a blueberry and find yourself chewing on little nutlike seeds, you're eating a huckleberry—one of the blueberry's close relatives.

If you climb mountains or tramp through bogs during the late weeks of summer, you'll find more blueberries than you can eat. The little clusters are so simple to pick, it's easy to keep reaching for yet another handful, and eating them this way invites fantasies of living off the land. A steady diet of blueberries would eventually take its toll on the human digestive system, but even so, while you're feasting and fantasizing it may be a good time to think about the earth's abundance—and the basic relationship between plants and animals that keeps us all alive.

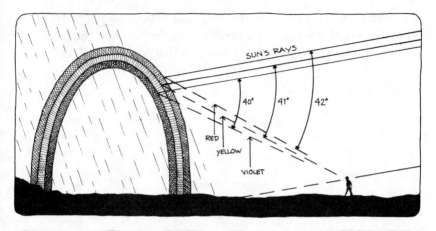

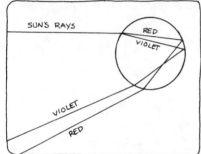
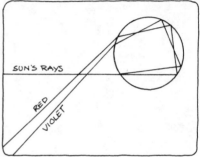

# RAINBOWS
## *Learning to Observe a Phenomenon of the Atmosphere*

*T*he basic ingredients of a rainbow are sun and rain—and human eyes to see what happens when one hits the other. When the white light of the sun hits raindrops, some of it passes through them, but some of it is also reflected back toward the viewer, separated into the seven different colors that make up sunlight. To understand exactly what happens, you have to visualize raindrops as little spheres; or maybe it's easier to think of them as circles. When the sunlight enters the front of the circle at just the right angle, it bends slightly and separates into its component colors. The colors then hit the back of the circle and are reflected forward again. When they emerge from the front of the raindrop, our eyes perceive the seven colors of the rainbow: red at the top, then orange, yellow, green, blue, indigo, and violet at the bottom.

Weather won't always cooperate and offer you a rainbow right when you want to see one, but on a sunny day you can use your garden hose to create one. You have to stand with the sun directly at your back, your shadow pointed straight in front of you, and the hose held so that in your shadow it looks like a geyser shooting out the top of your head. If you stand in the wrong position, or aim the hose too far to the left or right, you will lose most or all of your rainbow. You will also lose it if you aim the hose too low. It may take a bit of experimenting, but you should be able to produce a beautiful arc in the shower of falling water.

To understand why the rainbow is an arc, you have to imagine a straight line going from the sun through your head into the ground in front of you. This line points to the center of the circle of which the rainbow is the upper part. If you were standing high enough—on a tall building, or better yet, traveling in an airplane—you could see the whole circle. But since you're standing on the ground, the horizon, or if you're creating a rainbow with a hose, your lawn, cuts off the bottom part.

You can produce the best rainbows when the sun is fairly low in the sky. When the sun is low, the line through your head is tilted at a higher angle, and the rainbow's arc is more complete. You might even succeed in producing a second rainbow above the first. The second rainbow will be fainter, and its colors will be reversed—red at the bottom and violet at the top—because the light forming this second rainbow has a different relationship to the water droplet. It enters at the bottom of the droplet and reflects twice off the back of the circle before it comes out the front again. The second reflection inside the droplet both weakens the light and reverses the order of the colors.

As you experiment with the hose, you will learn that the rainbow itself stands still. The hose is like a beam of light that picks up the rainbow when you point it in the right direction. Even if you dance the spray up, down, and all around to see if you can make the rainbow move, the rainbow will stay right where it wants to be. That's because a rainbow involves precise angles of sunlight to water droplets to human eye, and anything other than those angles avoids the bendings and reflections that produce the arc of colors we see.

Some people might argue that a rainbow shouldn't be analyzed, but there's something powerful about the fact that human eyes are the meeting point where the sun acts on rain—or maybe it's the rain acting on the sun—to produce a seven-colored arc. The physical principles that explain why are more awe-inspiring than our most imaginative notions.

# MUSHROOMS
## *Learning to Look at Mushrooms*

$T$he world of mushrooms is an eerie and fascinating
place. When you walk in the fall woods, you might be surprised
by all the colors, shapes, and textures that seem to have sprung
suddenly from stumps, logs, and leaf litter. As a group, mushrooms have been credited with more powers than any other type
of plant. Legends record their ability to cause both miracle cures
and sudden deaths, with the possibility of cosmic visions in between. They are also known for their importance to witches'
brews, on the one hand, and their contributions to gourmet meals
on the other. Whereas many people seem to be interested in
which mushrooms they can eat to achieve specific effects, it's actually more important to understand what the mushrooms them-

selves are eating. But first, where does a mushroom come from, and what does its appearance mean?

Mushrooms begin life as tiny spores. A mushroom that you see is the spore-producing part of a mature plant, the rest of which is either underground or inside whatever the mushroom is growing out of. When you inspect the underside of the mushroom's cap, you will see either slits, called *gills*, or pin-sized holes, called *pores*. The spores are produced inside these openings and released from them when they are ripe. Each mushroom offers millions of microscopic spores to the wind, where they are circulated for a while and then dropped. Many of the spores will, of course, land in places where they can't grow, but sheer numbers guarantee that at least some of them will find the conditions they need to germinate.

When a mushroom spore finds a suitable place to grow, it begins the next stage of its life cycle by putting out a few fine hairs called *hyphae*. These hyphae grow inside the host material where they can't be seen. The first thing the tentative hyphae must do in order to produce a new mushroom is to find hyphae growing from another spore of the same species but of the opposite sex. Only when these two sets of hyphae unite can they proceed to grow into a plant that will eventually send up new mushrooms to distribute another generation of spores.

The fine hyphae grow into a dense and weblike mat called a *mycelium*. If you dig into whatever the mushroom is growing out of, you'll see some fine white webbing that represents part of the mycelium. It is the job of the mycelium to secrete enzymes and digest food for the growing plant. Eventually, the dense mass of hidden hyphae begins to form a special structure that will protrude above the ground or outside the tree or log, and that's when we see the familiar mushrooms that sometimes, after a fall rain, seem to pop up overnight.

While mushrooms are going about their own private business of eating and growing and reproducing their kind, they are also performing an important service to other living things. Mushrooms are *decomposers*, which means they break down, or decompose, the physical structures and chemical bonds that trap organic compounds in the bodies of plants and animals. As a byproduct of the mushroom's own life processes, it decomposes the material it lives in, returning elements and simple compounds to the soil to be used again. The appearance of so many mushrooms in the fall dramatizes nature's ongoing provisions for future life at a time when much of life seems to be dying, disappearing, or winding down for the cold days of winter that lie ahead.

# TOADS
## *Learning to Admire Toads*

*W*hen the weather turns cold, toads disappear. They dig themselves deep into the earth to spend the winter in hibernation. The timing of their disappearance is perfect, for the cold weather of fall also eliminates most of the insects toads feed on. Together, predator and prey respond to the seasons with the ancient strategies that perpetuate their species.

A toad's life might not seem very exciting, with half of it spent hibernating and much of the rest of it spent hiding, but researchers who have followed toads around in the field and observed them in the laboratory have discovered many clever and effective adaptations.

First, toads have succeeded in separating themselves more completely from water than most of their amphibian kin. Their skin is thicker and drier than the moisture-dependent skin of frogs. Except for the spring breeding period, when toads return to ancestral ponds to mate and lay their numerous eggs in long, gelatinous strings, they can make do with moist soil.

The American toad, which is common throughout most of the eastern United States and Canada, is perfectly colored, textured, and shaped for a terrestrial life. It is mottled with browns, tans, olive-greens, and rust-reds, and its dry, warty skin and chunky body make it look very much like a clump of earth. In gardens, where toads spend much of their time looking for insects and other invertebrates, they sometimes partially bury themselves to further camouflage their presence, and in the woods they blend right into the leaf litter.

Related to this protective coloration is the toad's ability to stay very still—or even to play dead—to avoid being perceived as live prey. But if the coloration and stationary posture fail and the toad finds itself in danger, it has several other tactics. It can hop—awkwardly, and without achieving the great distances managed by long-legged frogs—but with the same suddenness, which sometimes startles the predator. If hopping fails and the toad is caught in the predator's mouth, it exudes a poisonous substance from the large, bean-sized paratoid glands near its head and the smaller warts all over its body. This poison irritates mucous membranes and is strong enough to discourage most mammalian predators.

The number of large, fat toads you see during the summer is testimony to the effectiveness of toad defenses. But thousands of exceedingly small toadlets emerge from the mating ponds each year—usually after a soaking midsummer rain—and only a relative few of these grow to large, fat adulthood. So, many toads do indeed get eaten. Their chief enemies include snakes, hawks, owls, crows, and skunks.

Toads have another adaptation—or maybe it should be called a potential because it doesn't operate except in the laboratory. All males and some females have a small, undeveloped structure called a *Bidder's organ*, which can become a fully functional ovary if something happens to the toad's primary sex organs. Researchers have removed males' testes and found that even a mature male, who has fathered several years' worth of offspring, will respond by developing an ovary, producing eggs, and conducting him(her)self henceforth as a female. The young produced by this male-turned-female are normal toads capable of growing to adulthood and reproducing.

It's difficult to determine what advantage this Bidder's organ might give toads in the wild, but its presence and its potential do make toads of special interest to researchers. There's no question that toads, with their array of defenses and their ability to live away from water, feed on abundantly available insects, and hibernate through winter, are survivors. Maybe their Bidder's organ tells us something else about surviving—in the past or perhaps the future—that we haven't figured out yet.

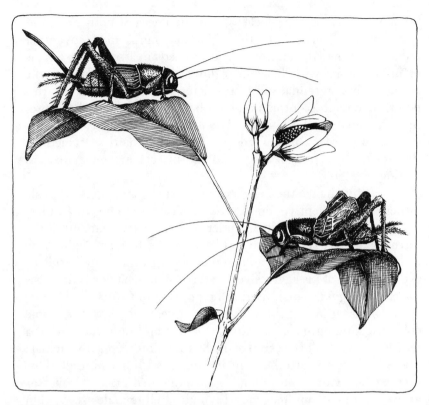

# FIELD CRICKETS
## Learning to Listen to Night Music

*F*ield crickets wait until fall to mate. The familiar *breeep* ... *breeep* ... *breeep* we hear coming from a grassy field, a stone wall, or the foundation of a building is the male field cricket's calling song. He uses these loud, jingly chirps, which he produces not with his voice but with his wings, to invite wandering females to his territory. A male cricket has crinkled little wings, both of which have a ridged vein called a *file* and a hardened section of the wing edge called a *scraper*. While both wings can either file or scrape, most field crickets are what researchers call "right-winged"—the right wing passes over the left, with the right file and left scraper producing the characteristic chirps.

The field cricket has more than these chirps in his repertoire, but human ears would have to listen very closely to hear them. Crickets' ears are located near the knees of both front legs and are very sensitive to the different sounds made by other members of their species. If a male succeeds in attracting a female to his territory with his loud calling song, he responds to the touch of her antennae with a quieter courtship song. At this point, touch and scent combine with sound to engage the appropriate behavior in both sexes. The long antennae that can be extended forward or backward and two other hairlike structures that look like a pair of tails help the insects maneuver toward mating.

If by chance the male's calling attracts an aggressive male rather than a receptive female, the musician switches to a different song. He warns off the intruder with a rivalry song, but if the intruder doesn't retreat, the resident male is ready to fight. One or both males might lose an antenna, leg, or other appendage, or even be killed. This aggressive and territorial behavior is the basis for cricket fights, which used to be popular in China.

Not all male field crickets are aggressive, however. Some enter the singing male's territory silently and hide there until a female arrives. This secretive male then intercepts the female who's heading toward the song and mates with her himself. This *satellite* behavior is not a choice an individual cricket makes or grows out of—it's in his genes. Enough satellite males succeed in mating that their genes are passed along, and the two modes of mating are represented generation after generation.

Even if either type of male is successful in mating, his genes are not assured of representation in the next generation. Sometimes the female receives the male's sperm packet, which he attaches to the outside of her body, but eats it before the sperm can fertilize her. Researchers theorize that the female's multiple matings might be less an expression of concern for the future generation than an expression of her present appetite.

But many females do get fertilized. The female, who can be distinguished from the male by her tidy, songless wings and her needlelike ovipositor, then lays several hundred eggs in the soil, where they will overwinter. Next spring, the young crickets will emerge, feed on vegetation, grow, and pass through eight to twelve molts. Their last molt will reveal wings and fully developed reproductive equipment, and the mating songs will begin again. The singing of a field cricket is a cheerful sound by itself, but as a part of the fall chorus of insect song, it's somewhat melancholy. These fall songs are dying sounds, the last gestures of creatures who must finish their life's work before the killing frost.

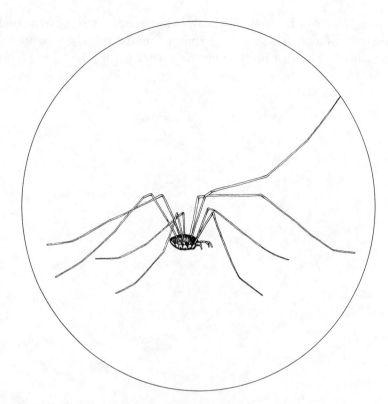

# DADDY LONGLEGS
*Learning to Observe an Arachnid
That Isn't a Spider*

*W*hen you're working outdoors on a fall day, you might feel the faintest tickle on your neck or the back of your hand. There's no buzz or squirm as there would be with an insect, nor is there the feeling of rapidly moving feet there would be with a spider. The sensation feels more like air than matter, but when you brush your neck or look at your hand, you'll find a living creature—a daddy longlegs.

A daddy longlegs is somewhat like a spider—they are both eight-legged animals classified as arachnids—but it is quite different in appearance and behavior. One of the most visible differences is the body shape. Whereas a spider has two distinct body parts—a cephalothorax and an abdomen—a daddy longlegs' body is all of a piece. Its cephalothorax and abdomen are joined to form a continuous oval shape.

Other differences are less visible. Spiders, for instance, have eight eyes, while daddy longlegs have only two. These two are located opposite each other on a small turret toward the front of the body. Spiders also have silk glands for spinning webs and poison glands for paralyzing prey. Daddy longlegs lack both, but manage to catch insects and other invertebrates just as effectively without them.

While daddy longlegs lack some of the equipment and resources of spiders, they have a few assets of their own. They have odor glands that emit a smell offensive to most of their predators, and they also have sex organs that permit direct copulation. Male spiders must transport their sperm to the female on the tip of an armlike appendage called a pedipalp.

The daddy longlegs' most prominent feature, as its common name implies, is its long legs. These legs look extremely fragile, but they serve the animal well. Each one is divided into seven segments, with numerous subsegments toward the tip. The segmentation enables the daddy longlegs to stand in its characteristic pose, body close to the ground, where it finds its prey, its long, bent legs surrounding it like great elbows. The long legs with the short subsegments toward the tips help the daddy longlegs move easily over rough and irregular terrain.

These legs are not just a means of locomotion, however. They are also an important part of the daddy longlegs' sensory equipment. The second pair are especially sensitive. When disturbed, or when merely exploring, the daddy longlegs waves this pair in the air to sense what's nearby. If one of these second legs is removed, the daddy longlegs is handicapped, but it can still function. If both of them are removed or lost, however, it will soon die.

Daddy longlegs are sometimes known as harvestmen because they appear so abundantly in the fall. They're active earlier in the summer, but they tend to hide low in the vegetation until they are full grown. Daddy longlegs hatch in the spring from eggs that were laid the prior fall. The young daddy longlegs molts about an hour after it hatches and then molts again seven or eight times at ten-day intervals, gaining a little more of its adult equip ment each time it sheds its skin. By fall, it is ready to mate. Daddy longlegs mate casually, with no preliminary courtship, and both sexes mate more than once with more than one partner. The female lays several batches of eggs in the soil, under a log, or in a crevice, and then she's ready to die. The males sometimes die even earlier than the females.

A daddy longlegs' life is short, but it accomplishes everything it needs to accomplish in one brief season. As the plants and animals around us make their preparations for winter, they confront us with a question: If a species' survival is just a matter of projecting its genes into the future, why do so many of us live on—active, inactive, semi-active through winter—to resume our activities in the spring? Other matters must enter in. Trees, turtles, and human beings gain some advantage from time that a daddy longlegs doesn't need.

# SHOOTING STARS
## Learning to Observe the Heavens

*A*s fall days shorten toward winter, an evening walk presents you with a sky full of stars. The familiar fixed points you are learning to recognize by position will be in their places—but suddenly a light that seems to come from nowhere shoots across the sky. As abruptly as it appeared, it disappears, leaving you wondering what would make a star shoot so unexpectedly across the sky? And what becomes of a star that has fallen out of place?

Anxiety is unwarranted. The phenomenon we call a "shooting star" isn't a star at all. It is actually a piece of interplanetary debris that has collided with the earth's atmosphere. The friction of this solid object moving at a high speed through the atmosphere causes the solid matter to glow with a white heat until it melts and vaporizes high above the earth. During the time it's visible, astronomers call it a meteor. If it doesn't vaporize completely and reaches the earth intact, it's then called a meteorite. "Shooting star" is just a misleading common name for one of these meteors on its way, perhaps, to becoming a meteorite.

Meteorites are important to scientists—and to us—because they provide clues to the formation of our solar system. Radioactive dating of meteorites indicates that they originated about 4.5 billion years ago, which is the time most scientists think our solar system was formed. Whereas the most familiar bodies in the solar system are the planets, which revolve in concentric, almost circular orbits around the sun, the solar system also contains fragments of solid matter called asteroids and mystery objects called comets.

The asteroids travel together in a doughnutlike formation called the asteroid belt, which is located between the orbits of Mars and Jupiter. This asteroid belt is almost on the same plane as the other planets, and the asteroids move in the same direction as the planets.

Comets are more independent. Their orbits are highly elongated, with the sun located near one end rather than in the middle. These orbits are pitched at random angles to the plane of the planets, and the comets, unlike the asteroids, are as likely to be moving against the planets as with them. The only time we see a comet is when it swings close to the sun—gaseous tail blowing in the solar wind and the whole phenomenon reflecting the sun's light. But by far the longer part of the comet's orbit takes it on a long and frigid journey to the edges of the solar system. Some comets travel so far that they fly outside the solar system and are lost in outer space. Others have fallen apart in orbit but continue to travel in the comet's former path as a stream of fragments.

Our shooting stars, or more accurately, our meteors, come from both the asteroid belt and from former comets. Sometimes asteroids collide, sending solid fragments through interplanetary space, where some of them hit the earth's atmosphere. These are the random meteors. Periodically, the earth also passes through the orbit of a former comet and encounters the stream of debris that is left. That's when we experience what astronomers call a meteor shower—a display that seems to radiate from a point among the stars, offering us a view of as many as forty to fifty meteors per hour.

So a shooting star is not a real star—a distant sun that might be supporting its own system of planets, asteroids, and comets—falling out of the familiar night sky. It is rather a fragment from our own solar system. Because each of these fragments is a potential clue to the mystery of the earth's origins, seeing a meteor is a hopeful, not an ominous, event. The order of the universe is not changing, diminishing, or falling apart. Evidence of a more recent and immediate event is merely entering the earth's atmosphere and offering itself to our understanding.

# READING SUGGESTIONS
# TO HELP YOU
# IN YOUR OBSERVATIONS

*I* write a weekly natural history column for several Vermont newspapers, which is my way of motivating, structuring, and sharing what I'm learning about the natural world. I have been involved in this enterprise for seven years now and have developed a regular pattern of exploration as I address myself to each week's subject.

I begin in the field with my own observations, descriptions, notes, and questions. While I'm still trying to figure out the name of what I've become interested in, or trying to get a basic understanding of it if I already know its name, I consult my growing collection of field guides. The Peterson Series, which is published by Houghton Mifflin, is standard. Some volumes in the series, like the *Field Guide to the Insects* and the *Field Guide to the Butterflies,* are too technical for me, but others, like the *Field Guide to Trees and Shrubs* and the *Field Guide to the Ferns,* offer very helpful keys.

I like the Peterson Series *Field Guide to the Birds* and *Field Guide to the Wildflowers* for their illustrations and the *Field Guide to Animal Tracks* for Olaus Murie's descriptions of what he saw in the field. *A Field Guide to Birds' Nests* and *A Field Guide to Edible Wild Foods* are also attractive, efficient, and easy to use.

The Golden Field Guides, published by The Golden Press, are colorful and cover all of North America rather than dividing it into eastern, western, or yet smaller geographic regions. The illustrations, range maps, and species descriptions are all together on facing pages. I prefer the convenience and color of the Golden Field Guides, but when I can't figure out the name of what I'm looking at, I find I have to rely on some of the Peterson Series keys. The titles I find most useful among the Golden Field Guides include *Birds of North America, Trees of North America, Amphibians of North America,* and *Reptiles of North America.*

The new Audubon Society Field Guides, published by Alfred A. Knopf, keep adding new titles. The front half of each of these field guides is filled with good quality color photographs, and the back half offers descriptive information and notes on habitat, range, life cycle, and such. The titles I have found especially useful so far are the *Field Guide to North American Insects and Spiders* and the *Field Guide to North American Butterflies.*

I cannot complete a discussion of field guides without reference to E. Laurence Palmer and H. Seymour Fowler's *Fieldbook of Natural History* (New York: McGraw-Hill Book Company, 1975), which includes thousands of common plants and animals in one volume, and Lawrence Newcomb's *Newcomb's Wildflower Guide* (Boston: Little, Brown and Company, 1977), which makes keying out wild flowers a game as well as a lesson in taxonomy. Also, Charles Roth's *The Wildlife Observer's Guidebook* (Englewood Cliffs, N.J.: Prentice-Hall, 1982) is handy to have.

When I have gone as far as I can with my own observations and the field guides, I travel to the Bailey-Howe Library at the University of Vermont, where I customarily spend at least half a day in the Reference Department. First, I consult all five of their general interest encyclopedias to get a sense of what's known about the subject I'm researching, Latin names, problems or issues I might want to focus on, clarifying illustrations, and words I might use later when I use the indexes. The five encyclopedias I sweep through include *Collier's* (1982 edition), *Americana* (1982 edition), *Academic American* (1982 edition), *World Book* (1982 edition), and the *Encyclopedia Britannica Micropedia* and *Macropedia* (1982 edition).

When I finish with the encyclopedias, I visit the reference shelves to see what some of the standard reference works have to say about my subject. If I am researching a flower, I generally start with Harold William Rickett's *Wild Flowers of the United States* (New York: McGraw-Hill Book Company, 1966). This is an oversized, fifteen-book set organized by geographic region. The color photographs are excellent, and Rickett offers brief information on every species of wild flower a generalist is likely to encounter.

After Rickett, I turn to the various lexicons, dictionaries, and manuals in the plant section of the reference collection. I find Robert Shosteck's *Flowers and Plants: An International Lexicon with Biographical Notes* (New York: Quadrangle/New York Times Book Company, 1974) useful for the meanings of Latin names and the origins of common names. J. C. Willis's *A Dictionary of the Flowering Plants and Ferns* (8th ed. Cambridge: The University Press, 1973) doesn't always make sense to me, but it sometimes offers interesting information on the flower's structure, pollination strategy, and pollinators.

I find Henry A. Gleason and Arthur C. Cronquist's *Manual of Vascular Plants* (New York: D. Van Nostrand Company, Inc., 1963) almost incomprehensible, but with the help of a botanical dictionary I can make use of their technical information to visualize the exact flower structure. The botanical dictionaries I rely on are John R. Little and C. Eugene Jones's *A Dictionary of Botany* (New York: Van Nostrand Reinhold Company, 1980), which is quite technical, and Michael Chinery's *A Science Dictionary of the Plant World* (New York: Franklin Watts, Inc., 1969), which is a colorful, profusely illustrated general interest dictionary.

For plants that are edible, I check the reference books on edible wild foods. I find a recent book by Joan Richardson especially appealing. Her *Wild Edible Plants of New England* (Yarmouth, Maine: DeLorme Publishing Company, 1981) is clear, interesting, and attractive. Bradford Angier's *Field Guide to Edible Wild Plants* (Harrisburg, Pennsylvania: Stackpole Books, 1974) offers decent color illustrations and brief information on facing pages. The Dover reprint of Mrs. M. Grieve's *A Modern Herbal* (2 vols., New York: Dover Publications, Inc., 1971) offers good background information on medicinal plants and includes exact amounts that should be used for different remedies. Ben Charles Harris's *The Compleat Herbal* (Barre, Massachusetts: Barre Publishers, 1972) discusses the Doctrine of Signatures and explains how each plant relates to that fascinating doctrine.

If I'm researching a tree, I consult Thomas S. Elias's *The Complete Trees of North America* (New York: Van Nostrand Reinhold Company, 1980) and R. C. Hosie's *Native Trees of Canada* (8th ed., Don Mills, Ontario: Fitzhenry and Whiteside Ltd., 1979). Elias offers range maps for all the species and diagnostic illustrations of leaves, flowers, and fruits or seeds, while Hosie offers silhouettes and black and white photographs of buds, leaf scars, flowers, seeds, bark, and leaves.

If I happen to be working on an animal rather than a plant, the reference collection offers other titles. I generally start with Bernhard Grzimek's *Grzimek's Animal Life Encyclopedia* (New York: Van Nostrand Reinhold Company, 1972). This thirteen-volume set is comprehensive, international, and offers a bit of information on just about every animal you can imagine. I have, however, found a few inaccuracies.

For insects, my favorite reference work is Lester A. Swan and Charles S. Papp's *The Common Insects of North America* (New York: Harper and Row Publishers, 1972). They focus on just the common insects, which are the ones I usually notice, offer clear black and white illustrations, and frequently explain the insect's life cycle. Walter Linsenmaier's *Insects of the World* (New York: McGraw-Hill Book Company, 1972) includes some interesting information, but because the author is European, he ignores a lot of the common North American insects.

For ready reference on birds, the best thing that's happened in recent history is the publication of John K. Terres's *The*

*Audubon Society Encyclopedia of North American Birds* (New York: Alfred A. Knopf, 1980). Terres refers to the latest research on each species and includes an extensive bibliography for further reading. Terres is not as chatty and charming as A. C. Bent and associates, who compiled a twenty-six volume treatment of North American birds between the 1930s and 1960s, but he brings all the species up to date and offers a convenient, single-volume reference.

Two older books I enjoy consulting because they offer good field descriptions are Frank M. Chapman's *Handbook of Birds of Eastern North America* (New York: Dover Publications, Inc., 1966) and Edward Howe Forbush and John Bichard May's *A Natural History of American Birds of Eastern and Central North America* (Boston: Houghton Mifflin Company, 1939).

When I am researching a mammal, I always consult Alfred J. Godin's *Wild Mammals of New England* (Baltimore: The Johns Hopkins University Press, 1977; paperback edition, 1982) because he offers a review of what is known about each species and a complete bibliography of scholarly research for each genus. William J. Hamilton, Jr. and John O. Whitaker, Jr.'s *Mammals of the Eastern United States* (2nd ed. Ithaca: Comstock Publishing Associates/Cornell University Press, 1979) is less formal and more readable. The two books are complementary.

When I am researching a constellation or celestial phenomenon, I am in over my head from the start, but I have discovered a few reference books that are helpful. Most of them are alphabetical dictionaries with very brief information on lots of subjects. The books I usually consult include David F. Tver's *Dictionary of Astronomy, Space, and Atmospheric Phenomena* (New York: Van Nostrand Reinhold Company, 1979), Valerie Illingworth (ed.)'s *The Facts on File Dictionary of Astronomy* (New York: Facts on File, 1979), Simon Mitton (ed.)'s *The Cambridge Encyclopedia of Astronomy* (2nd ed., London: Adam Hilger, 1976). I also like Chet Raymo's *365 Starry Nights: An Introduction to Astronomy for Every Night of the Year* (Englewood Cliffs, N.J.: Prentice-Hall, 1982).

After surveying the reference books, I dig into the indexes. The most useful index for unearthing scholarly treatments of the plants and animals I am researching is the *Biological and Agricultural Index.* This multivolume index lists articles in journals not covered by popular indexes. Some of these journals, which I have come to depend on for exhaustive studies or up-to-date information, include the *American Journal of Botany, American Midland Naturalist, American Naturalist, American Zoologist, Animal Behaviour, Annals of the Entomological Society of America, Annual Review of Entomology, Auk, Canadian Journal of Botany, Canadian Journal of Plant Science, Canadian Journal of Zoology, Condor, Ecology, Economic Botany, Journal of Insect Physiology, Journal of Mammalogy, Journal of Zoology,* and *Plant Physiology.*

The *General Science Index,* which is a new index that has been available since 1978, covers many of the same journals as the *Biological and Agricultural Index,* but it also includes popular publications such as *Audubon, The Conservationist, Horticulture, National Wildlife,* and *Natural History.* It also covers astronomy and geology.

Finally, just to be sure I'm not overlooking anything current in a popular magazine, I look through the *Readers' Guide to Periodical Literature.* Occasionally *National Geographic, Organic Gardening, Science,* or *Smithsonian* has a useful article that the other indexes wouldn't have picked up.

One last reference resource is the card catalog. By the time I have looked through all the encyclopedias, reference books, and indexes, I know exactly what words to look up in the subject section of the card catalog and whose names to look for in the author-title section to see if they have written books. The rest of my research consists of reading through what I find interesting in the journals, magazines, textbooks, and specialized books.

I must acknowledge one last book, which I always save until last because it pulls me out of the deeply scientific back into the general, popular, and accessible. Anna Botsford Comstock's *Handbook of Nature Study* (24th ed., Ithaca: Comstock Publishing Associates/Cornell University Press, 1967) frequently offers me a descriptive detail, a field observation, an image, or a vision that shapes the way I think about the subject I have just discovered.

# APPENDIX I: *Contents by Life Form*

*Nonliving Things*
Frost
Orion
Cassiopeia
Rainbows
Shooting Stars

*Nonflowering Plants*
Ferns
Evergreen Ferns
Moss
Mushrooms

*Weeds, Wild Flowers,*
*and Other Flowering Plants*
Asters
Poison Ivy
Phragmites
Mistletoe
Poinsettias
Christmas Cactus
Ragweed
Trailing Arbutus
Violets
Pink Lady's Slippers
Stinging Nettles
Daisies and Black-Eyed Susans
Peppermint
Milkweed
Indian Pipes
Thistles
Goldenrods
Blueberries

*Trees*
Acorns
Fall Foliage
American Elm
Christmas Trees
Beech Trees
Maples

*Miscellaneous Life Forms*
Crayfish

*Arachnids*
Daddy Longlegs

*Insects*
Bumblebees
Monarch Butterflies
Bark Beetles
Mourning Cloak Butterflies
Black Flies
Water Striders
Whirligig Beetles
Honeybees
Deer Flies
Viceroy Butterflies
Spittlebugs
Inchworms
June Beetles
Bald-Faced Hornets
Field Crickets

*Amphibians*
Tadpoles
Bullfrogs
Toads

*Reptiles*
Painted Turtles
Garter Snakes
Snapping Turtles

*Birds*
Canada Geese
Mallards
Crows
Ravens
Snow Buntings
Starlings
Chickadees
Blue Jays
Great Horned Owls
Pigeons
Red-Winged Blackbirds
Sparrows
Northern Orioles

Grackles
Ruby-Throated Humming-
    birds
Herring Gulls
Mourning Doves
Cardinals

*Mammals*
    Gray Squirrels
    Black Bears
    Raccoons
    Skunks
    Wolves
    Eastern Coyotes

# APPENDIX II: Related Chapters

*Plant Evolution*
  Moss
  Ferns

*Fungi*
  American Elm
  Mushrooms

*Composites*
  Asters
  Daisies and Black-Eyed Susans
  Thistles
  Goldenrods

*Pollination Strategies*
  Asters
  Poinsettias
  Ragweed
  Trailing Arbutus
  Violets
  Pink Lady's Slippers
  Ruby-Throated Humming-
    birds
  Milkweed
  Thistles
  Goldenrods
  Blueberries

*Flies*
  Black Flies
  Deer Flies

*Beetles*
  Bark Beetles
  Whirligig Beetles
  June Beetles

*Butterflies and Moths*
  Monarch Butterflies
  Mourning Cloak Butterflies
  Viceroy Butterflies
  Inchworms

*Social Insects*
  Bumblebees
  Honeybees
  Bald-Faced Hornets

*Imports and Camp Followers*
  Starlings
  Pigeons

*Indoor Subjects*
  Mistletoe
  Poinsettias
  Christmas Cactus
  Christmas Trees

*Edible Wild Foods*
  Stinging Nettles
  Peppermint
  Milkweed
  Blueberries

*Aquatic Species*
  Canada Geese
  Mallards
  Painted Turtles
  Phragmites
  Tadpoles
  Black Flies
  Water Striders
  Whirligig Beetles
  Crayfish
  Deer flies
  Bullfrogs
  Snapping Turtles
  Herring Gulls

*Parasites*
  Mistletoe

*Pigeon Family*
  Pigeons
  Mourning Doves

# INDEX